CAR
BUYERS
HAND
BOOK

by

Skip Thomsen
and
Cathleen Freshwater

TABLE OF CONTENTS

Introduction 5

1. Avoiding the Squeeze 9

2. Private-party Sales 30

3. The "Book" and Its Mystery Unraveled 35

4. Dealer Auctions and Salvage Pools 40

5. The "FTC" Sticker 47

6. Warranties 51

7. Insurance 57

8. Trade-ins 67

9. Financing 71

10. Deciding What You Need 76

11. Miles per Gallon vs. Miles per Dollar 104

12. Planned Obsolescence 113

13. Special Interest Cars 125

14. Check It Out—Body 138

15. Check It Out—Mechanical 151

16. The Test Drive 168

17. What to Do When It Breaks 176

18. Conclusion 199

Index 203

Acknowledgments

We thank all the dealers, both scrupulous and nefarious, with whom we have dealt in the last few decades for their contributions, both conscious and unknowing. We couldn't have done it without you, nor would there have been any need.

Limits of Liability and Disclaimer

The authors of this book have used their best efforts in its preparation, which include not only the experience gained in their collective 35 years in the automobile business and their personal expertise, but also the feedback of countless business associates, customers, and friends. The authors shall not be liable in any event for incidental or consequential damages in connection with or arising out of the use of the information contained in this book.

"He" includes "she" in all cases except the specific.

ISBN 0-9625960-2-7

INTRODUCTION

For over 25 years we earned our keep in the used-car market. We maintained our integrity by offering only quality cars for sale. Autos that we would, and did, let our mothers drive.

We daily witnessed marketing practices ranging from barely legal deceit, to trickery, to downright dishonesty. Advertising techniques, devious in almost every arena, are especially so in the automobile trade.

In the marketplace we saw automobiles of such dubious reliability, even cars which had been obviously and shoddily rebuilt from wrecks, that we wondered how they could be sold. Who would buy anything so poorly trashed together, so ill prepared for the open road? Not only buy, but pay more than they should have for a premium example of the same car.

Yet there was no shortage of buyers. The dealers of these lemons were making piles of money. Where did their customers come from? Why were they blind to the obvious defects? Why were they so easily preyed upon by salesmen with unscrupulous tactics?

It's all part of the game.

Most people decide to buy a car when they think they need a change. Maybe the old ride is wearing out, or they have outgrown its usefulness: a new baby, a new job, a new divorce, or maybe they just see a spot on TV. Something inspires a desire for change.

Yet very few buyers manage to satisfy their actual needs with their next car. Car buyers have been conditioned to make buying a car an emotional experience rather than a purchase of goods. They have no idea to what lengths a car salesman will go to coerce them into making a purchase of his choosing.

After observing even our own friends and relatives (who should have known better) fall victim to auto hustling, we decided to do something about it. We were sure we could teach them to become consumers who can make intelligent decisions in a complicated process. We would show them how to sidestep a system designed by experts to misrepresent, intimidate, and force them to buy whatever the industry is offering.

Certainly not all used cars are defective, but all used cars have flaws. Many new cars have flaws, But disguising defects is only one of the games dealers play. Others involve manipulations in the sales office which cause customers to pay thousands of dollars more for their purchase than was originally implied.

Dealers' games are standard industry practice. Auto dealers conduct seminars and intensive training workshops to teach their sales people these profit oriented programs. Over the years, these training practices have been fine tuned by professional psychologists skilled in the intricacies of the buying mind. Against this kind of training, Mr. and Mrs. Joe Average haven't a chance.

But you can change the way you buy cars. You can avoid falling in love in the showroom with some four-wheeled floozy you wind up married to for the length of the contract. You can make intelligent decisions before you enter the market. You can stay within set parameters to find the car you need. And you can do it within your budget.

We're doing our part by writing this book. We don't include lists of all of the cars of recent years which have proven to be lemons. There are already books available which offer this information in other presentations. It might be more to the point and less confusing to ask your mechanic for his opinion of a particular make and model that interests you. Do you really want to memorize a huge table of all of the defective, or potentially defective cars, engines, and transmissions on the market?

Wouldn't you rather learn to detect deception in any car you consider purchasing?

Then you do your part by reading through these pages and by following their tested advice. We have kept *Car Buyers Hand Book* conversational and informative so that, together, we can change the car-dealing climate.

Use this book as a guide to the automobile market. Be prepared for things that are not as they seem: Dealers who smile sweetly while they lie and intimidate to make a sale, and cars that look like something they are not.

Decide what you want before you go shopping. Do not wait to be convinced in the candy store atmosphere of the showroom that what you really want is the shiny red sports model the salesman is polishing.

And lest you be frightened completely out of the market, be assured that there are honest dealers and good cars available. You can find them once you know how to look.

Skip Thomsen
Cathleen Freshwater

1. AVOIDING THE SQUEEZE

Even the sanest, most rational, most conservative person has difficulty keeping his emotions out of his decision to buy a car. There's just something about cars that wants to be bought.

Think about your last purchase. Did you decide that, based upon the number of people in your family, you would need so many doors? Because you drive so many miles per year, you need so many miles per gallon? That manual transmissions yield better fuel mileage or that yellow is the safest color? Did you then compute what kind of a car you should buy?

Did the appearance of the car enter the picture? Did you consider that if you bought the econo-model, your friends and neighbors would think you couldn't afford a decent car?

Few people ever buy a car without projecting a

mental picture of themselves showing up somewhere in their new ride. Americans identify with their car, some more than others. Some are hard pressed to admit it. But even the most reluctant will concede that it feels better to drive a fine car than to motor about in a clunker.

Almost all auto purchases are emotional decisions. Rarely is a personal or family car bought rationally. Take a look at the ads. How do car makers advertise their products? Do they tell you how good their cars are? Do they give you any specifications or other details to demonstrate their worth?

No. They show you how much sex appeal you will generate by being associated with their merchandise. Or if you happen to belong to a different demographic group, they'll show you how you can one-up your business associates with their longer and wider than last year's model. Contemporary advertising addresses only one idea: that whatever you already have isn't good enough.

Every salesman knows, lives and breathes the certainty that emotion is the most powerful sales tool in his bag. They are aware of the necessity to control the buyer's emotions, so the most successful salesmen know more about psychology than they do about automobiles.

When we speak of "salesmen," we refer to women as well. Women make very effective auto salesmen. Seminar speakers often address the specific potentials an attractive woman has for selling vehicles. We know one woman who has a great deal of fun selling four-wheel drive rigs to men. The more macho the guy, the more fun she

10

has, and the greater the likelihood of a sale. She knows little about cars, but she is an expert at manipulation and intimidation.

And most dealers prefer that their sales people be auto-illiterate. Knowing a lot about the product just gets in the way of selling it. A good salesman doesn't sell the product, he sells himself. These words, by the way, are not ours. They are high-lighted in sales manuals in every field.

Remember to be aware that the decision to buy a car is rarely rational. You may argue that since the old car is getting tired and needs repairs, you might as well replace it. Or that you need more room or better mileage. But more often than not, the rationalizations are less than rational.

John and Mary Andersonsmith, a young couple with a baby on the way, decided they needed a station wagon. They spent hours gazing at sales brochures. Then they went to a slick dealer who talked them into buying a flashy two-seater for twice their decided dollar limit.

Why?

Because they went shopping unprepared for the assault on their sensibilities that they encountered in the candy store atmosphere of the showroom. We would like to share with you more real (though disguised) examples from a dealership where one of us worked for a couple of months, learning how cars were sold. Many of our customers were young couples who owned, free and clear, an older but dependable car.

Take the Johnsons, who talked themselves into shopping for a new car because rising fuel prices had made their old car with its poor gas mileage seem too expensive to operate. They justified a purchase and they drove away in a shiny new car. Unfortunately, they were run through the system and saddled with a debt load far beyond their budget. On their newly acquired debt, the interest payments alone would have bought the gas for their old, paid for car.

They soon realized that they owed more on their no-longer-new car than they could possibly sell it for. Soon they could no longer afford the payments. What were their options?

They could have gotten a high-interest, finance company loan to pay the difference between what they could sell the car for and what they owed on it. But that would have meant making payments to a finance company for a car they no longer owned. Or they could have let it be repossessed and ruin their credit rating.

But if they had not been sold a car that cost more than they could pay, they would have avoided their dilemma.

"When you buy a car you're not merely buying transportation, you are buying a lifestyle."

There need not be anything wrong with letting emotions play a part in the car selection process. But you must recognize the emotional pull—and control it. Not recognizing your emotional involvement allows the professional, highly trained salesman to get the upper hand, and keep it.

So, for your own valid reasons, you have decided to buy a new (or "new" used) car. No matter where you intend to shop, knowing what you are looking for makes it easier to keep a clear head. This is the best preventive for buyer's remorse.

The most obvious decisions are, of course, whether to go with a sedan, wagon, sports car, pickup, etc. (See Chapter 10 to help you evaluate your basic criteria.) Determine the guidelines you want to follow before you enter the marketplace and stick to them. Don't let a sharp salesman sell you something other than what you know you want.

Remember that buying a car is rarely a rational decision. Knowing it and believing it is the foundation for making an intelligent automobile purchase. The salesman knows it, and he puts it to work when he first sees you enter the parking lot.

Their training system instills in the minds of the sales force the notion that they are indeed the most important element in the entire order of the automotive world. If it were not for their valiant efforts, no cars would ever be sold. An ailing auto market would put hundreds of thousands of people out of work in this country alone. It's hard to imagine what a dismal world this would be, were it not for auto sales . . . .

So remember, when a salesman asks you your name, he is not just trying to be friendly. He's trying to control. Salesmen are trained to "use the prospect's name to put him at ease." He will call you by your name to convince you that he cares about you, but it's just part of his system.

Most professional car salesmen, particularly the ones working in franchised dealer's stores, are intensively trained within this system. They will keep nodding at you like bobbing corks to encourage a positive response.

A seasoned professional will continue to sell the car by relating only those qualities that fulfill the personal clues that you give him. For example, if you have four children and your primary concern is safety, he will show you statistics that point to the crash protection offered by a larger car. But if your opening remarks concern economy, he will show you a more compact model that will get better mileage and maybe even cost less to begin with.

Rarely will you be offered contradicting but positive features so that you can make your own decision. A well-trained salesman will not relinquish that much control to his customer, or "mark," as the customer is called in some training seminars. The salesman is much more interested in the number of units he can sell than in helping his customers make a practical purchase.

He also knows that if he sells himself, his mark will be so tickled at having met and made friends with such a great guy that he will be happy with his purchase. Even if the car turns out to be a lemon, the salesman is not likely to be blamed.

Here is a cursory outline of techniques taken directly from sales seminars:

1. Greet the customer warmly when he/she enters the showroom.

2. Give a hearty "Welcome" with a firm handshake to put him at his ease.

3. Establish control. Phrase questions very carefully to remove the option of saying, "No," or, "Just looking." (Example: "How may I help you?" The buyer's response is being framed in the salesman's favor.)

4. Get on a first name basis to lower the customer's guard and use the customer's name regularly in the conversation.

5. Give a business card so the customer can recall your name. It puts him at ease if he doesn't have to fret about having forgotten the name of someone so friendly.

6. Work the "hinge": keep nodding to encourage agreement.

7. Offer premature "Congratulations" to instill the idea of ownership.

8. Pay careful attention to smoking: smoke if he does, don't if he doesn't.

9. Never discuss the price of the car.

10. Turn your customer over to the next in line the instant you feel yourself losing control.

To control the situation, the salesman needs to discover your main reason for wanting to buy a car. He asks particular questions to ferret out that reason. And if he finds which of your buttons is most effective to push, he may just be able to unload that unsalable Juicemobile in the corner.

He phrases his questions very carefully, always assuming that you, the buyer, are already sold:

"Why are you looking for a new car today?"

If you tell him directly, he will know directly where to steer you to make his pitch most effective.

"What's most important to you in a new car?"

If you say, "Price," he will ask, "Yes, but other than the price?"

"Who's the new car going to be for?"

The clever salesman already has you thinking about the person(s) you will be disappointing if you don't go through with this sale.

"Where will you be taking your first trip in your new car?"

Now you'll be thinking about showing up at Cousin Ed's in that new ride. Note the part about ". . . your new car." It's already yours, right?

"Who else will be proud of the fact that you now own this car?"

In the first place, you don't own it yet. Secondly, the salesman is assuming that you are buying a car to make yourself proud. "Who else will be proud" is to set you to thinking of all of the people you will impress with your new car. This simple technique works well enough on most folks to close the sale.

"Is this car going to be for a special occasion, an anniversary or a birthday, or are you just rewarding yourself(ves)?"

Now, how will you tell this nice man that you might not even buy today? His approach has made it impossible not to buy without losing face.

The dealership mentioned earlier in this chapter where we got our first-hand experience was what is known as a "T-O House." "T-O" stands for turn over, the name of the system. We stayed there only long enough to see how the T-O system worked. Here is a simplified description of the basics.

Please remember that, although the names are fiction, the story is true.

When an "up" (another designation for customer) came on the lot, Harvey Handshake approached her with his well-rehearsed pitch. If for any reason, maybe she didn't like his red hair, or his style of speech, he felt that he was no longer in control of the circumstances, he turned her over to George Gladhand, who just happened (as a part of the system) to be standing inconspicuously nearby. By turning over the deal, Harvey had also split the commission, should George make a sale.

If George also found himself losing control of his customer, he again turned her over to strategically placed John Sincere. The commission would take another split.

Often, a couple would come onto the lot after work and wander around and look over the inventory with Harvey or George in hot pursuit. And the T-O team would coerce them, brainwash them, argue with them, and do whatever was necessary, even if it took until two o'clock the next morning, to sell them a car; sell them a car they would.

Their games were so effective that the salesmen often forced the buyers into a position in which one of them would threaten divorce if the car wasn't bought. Or they would back the stronger of the two into a corner from which he (or she) had but two choices: either sign the contract, or admit in front of the spouse to being deficient in the eyes of the salesmen.

One item of interest: not once, in our time of dealing with hundreds of customers in the T-O house, did we ever hear anyone ask what the full price of the car was. Not once. All they cared about were the "down" and monthly payments, making themselves easy prey.

It was standard practice, and still is in many dealerships, to con the "up" out of the keys to his car immediately upon getting him into the "box" (the little sales cubicles in most dealerships). Getting a customer's car keys was incredibly easy: "Our appraiser is here, so let's just have him check out your car and get that out of the way . . . ."

Why did Harvey Handshake want the keys? The keys are one of the most effective controls in the business. Example: The "up" was in the "box". He'd been there for five hours and six different salesmen had had their turns with him. He was frazzled, having had to deal with each salesman's spiel and piles of paperwork.

John Sincere had instructed him to fill out a long, involved form which said that he promised that he would, in fact, buy the car if the terms could be made to his approval. John had intimated that he didn't dare bring in such a low offer to his boss without having a promise that the customer wasn't just window shopping. Of course his boss, Harold Hardsell, had been listening in to the entire transaction over the intercom system which was hidden behind the picture on the wall in the "box."

If John began losing what control he still had, Mr. Hardsell would come in and tell John that his mother was on the phone and it sounded pretty important. That was the salesman's cue to get lost. Then Hardsell would start in on the guy. Hardsell was a real pro. Nobody walked on the boss.

Hardsell would probably close the sale in a short time, If he had any trouble, or if the customer got really mad and said he was just going to drive out, Hardsell would look surprised and, with a straight face, tell the guy that he didn't understand. "Drive out? Why we've already wholesaled your car . . . remember that form you signed? You don't have a car any more, buddy."

Of course, he hadn't really wholesaled the customer's car, that was just another lie. But the car had been locked up in the warehouse down the street that was kept for just this purpose.

Another common maneuver, if a deal was close at hand, was to ask the customer if there was anything about the prospective purchase that needed attention: any repairs or adjustments that could be made which would make the difference. Of course, almost any customer, when offered such a choice, will go for it. So George breaks out the special "Customer's Authorization for Repairs" and fills in all the blanks.

"We'll adjust the brakes, fix the radio, replace the rear tires, and straighten that little ding in the fender. Sure thing. Just sign here." He would fill out the form with all the repairs that the customer requested, have the customer sign it, and then give it to him.

What did the customer then have in hand? A piece of paper with his own signature on it. Nowhere on the form was the name of the dealership. Nowhere did any representative of the dealership sign the form. It was useless. But the customer liked it and it would often sell the car.

When the customer asked when and where the

repairs were to be done, George was trained with the perfect answer: "Fred," the house mechanic, was recovering from surgery and would be back at work in a week or two, so bring the car back then. Any customer query about the where abouts of Fred was a cue to tell why Fred wasn't available just now.

Fred didn't exist.

The customer would usually get tired of the game in a month or two and quit. On the rare occasion that a customer got wise and threatened to sue the house for the repairs, he needed only to be reminded that he had nothing which said the dealership owed him any repairs. None of the salesmen had ever even seen that form before, "Where did that come from?"

If these stories sound too bizarre to believe, be advised that this kind of treachery goes on in even some of the best-looking dealerships. We know stories which make these seem tame. Highway Robbery, published in 1966, is full of them. And not much has changed since then. The May, 1989, issue of *Los Angeles Magazine* carried an article entitled "Tales out of Car-Salesman School" which was reprinted in the January, 1990, *Reader's Digest.* Some newspapers still carry horror stories of buying cars. But according to the May 20, 1991, issue of *Newsweek*, automobile advertisers may well be stifling television news coverage of dealers' games and manipulations.

Our point is not to relate stories of what has happened before and is happening now at some level in many dealerships around the country. We want to arm you with enough information so that you can evade the traps long before they become dangerous.

We would like to offer you these protective guidelines when shopping for a car. Treat them as hard, fast rules:

NEVER, NEVER DISCUSS TRADE-INS
WITH A DEALER.

NEVER, NEVER DRIVE YOUR CAR
ONTO A DEALER'S LOT.

NEVER, NEVER DISCUSS FINANCING
WITH A DEALER.

ALWAYS ARRANGE YOUR FINANCING ON YOUR
OWN; TREAT YOUR PURCHASE AS A CASH SALE.

LEAVE YOUR CHECK BOOK AT HOME.

PARK FAR ENOUGH AWAY THAT THE SALES FORCE
DOES NOT SEE YOU GET OUT OF YOUR CAR.

AVOID "HARMLESS" CONVERSATION WITH THE
SALESMAN.

Asking around, which we recommend so highly when searching for a mechanic, cannot always be relied on when looking for a car dealer. Particularly not a new-car dealer, and that includes his used-car store. We have known more than a few reasonable, rational, intelligent adults who became victims of a highly skilled sales staff.

Smoothly manipulated through the whole operation, and obligated to an impossible contract on a car they neither needed nor wanted, they blamed partners, spouses, or friends for making "the stupid decision to buy this damn car." They rarely blamed the salesman.

It never occurred to them that they had been victimized by a staff of people highly trained in psychological warfare, not only were they highly trained in their specialized craft, but constantly retrained to keep them at their best.

How can a person who buys only one car every few years hope to prevail against such an opponent? The odds against the buyer are magnified when he has to face not just one salesperson, but a whole crew of sales people. If the first salesman should get the notion that he is no longer in complete control, the next one magically appears to take over.

Sound like an impossible situation? Well, there are ways to deal with it. If you are shopping for a used car, you have two options: buy from a private-party, and we will delve into the advantages of private-party shopping in the next chapter, or find a reasonable dealer.

Your chances of finding a dealer with whom you can work are increased if you restrict your search to independent dealers. That clearly excludes the used-car departments of most new-car stores. Most new-car stores have to run each customer and each sale through the system.

Even if you go onto the lot looking at an old pickup truck which ought to sell for $1,200, you will be subjected to the same barrage of intimidation that you would meet if you were looking at a new car on the showroom floor. You will not likely get a straight answer out of anyone about anything, including the price of the pickup.

If you decide to circumvent some of the rigmarole by asking to talk directly to the used-car sales manager, you will first be sized-up for gullibility by the professional who greets you. He may decide to tell you that he is in fact the manager. Or, if he doesn't think you'll buy that, he will call the turn-over man hiding in the shadows and introduce him to you as the manager you seek.

Many managers pride themselves in their rarely having to lower themselves to face a "mark." A manager's inaccessibility is a direct consequence of the proficiency of his sales force. This is the way it works at many new-car stores, and it's all part of the system.

Once you are aware of what goes on in a T-O system house, you should be able to recognize it if you walk into one.

If you do, immediately tell the first salesman who comes up to you that you are just looking for your dog and, no, you really have no use for a car. Tell him you can't even get a driver's license because of your frequent undiagnosable fainting spells, and you can't go to another doctor because they all know about your recent bankruptcy, and has he seen your dog? No? Adios.

Remember that there are exceptions. There are new-car stores where you can talk to someone who has the authority to sell you a car without going through a system-sell. It is possible in such a dealership to converse rationally with the salesperson, and/or the manager, and to buy a vehicle without a mind-boggling bunch of red tape.

But we can think of only a few. It is just easier to deal with independents.

Here's the bad news: there are also independents who utilize the same system-sell procedures. Many of these independents were trained in a new-car store and worked there long enough to realize that if they ran their own operation, they would no longer have to deal with management's manipulation of the figures that cheated the sales staff out of most of their commissions. Yes, there is thievery even within the den of thieves.

Ready for some good news? System-house independent dealers are usually easy to recognize. First, an unusually large used-car operation is suspect. As are several sales people on the place. A non-system independent will usually consist of two sales people at most on staff. If asked the price of a particular unit, a non-system salesman will give you a direct answer in dollars. This is one of the first things that the system-sell folks are taught never to do.

If a T-O house seller does finally give a dollar figure, it will be at least $1,000 over the price at which they would actually sell the car. This gives the house two immediate advantages: testing the buyer's reaction and naivete, and creating built-in headroom for manipulating figures when they get him in the box.

Favorable referrals are valid in checking an independent. Especially if you talk to several people who all feel that they were treated well. If any of these folks can relate a favorable after-the-sale story, such as the dealer's taking care of a problem beyond his legal obligation, that dealer is your best bet. It does happen.

Rural communities often offer better chances to find reputable independent dealers. A real con man will have difficulty staying alive for any length of time in a small community, and will certainly not be able to produce any repeat business referrals. Most rural dealers also have less overhead than dealers in the middle of the city. Some will pass the savings on to their customers. Others will only advertise that they do.

Some used-car dealers have large inventories that never seem to remain the same. Do their ever changing inventories mean that they are really moving the merchandise at what must be good prices? Not necessarily. These dealers may well just make more wholesale sales than retail.

Many dealers buy whole truckloads of cars at distant auctions and resell them at auctions nearer to home. These dealers profit by staying on top of the changing trends in auto values. (See Chapter 4, "Dealer Auctions.") Such a dealership is likely to be a better place to shop than a dealership whose inventory remains static, but not because of the anticipated lower prices. A wholesaler may just be too busy to bother playing games.

If you want an effective research program to find referrals other than those the dealer supplies, find a few people sporting license frames carrying local dealers' names, and ask them about the dealer where they bought their car. Grocery store parking lots are excellent sources for finding cars and their owners.

Once you've found a dealership to browse, remember that the best technique to employ when dealing with an auto salesman is to pretend you are at a hardware store looking for a tool you need. The salesman has no need and no right to know your life history. He has no legitimate reason to ask you for any personal information whatsoever. You ask him about the car.

Start by asking a few questions to which you already know the answers (technical stuff works well), to see if he knows anything about the car he's selling. If you find out that he knows less than you do, you have eliminated any possible reason to talk with him about anything at all.

Examine the car to your satisfaction. Bring along a knowledgeable friend and discuss it with him, not with the salesman. If the salesman insists on interjecting useless conversation in a continuing effort to sell you, leave and try another dealer. Whatever you do, never give a salesman a straight answer to any question which seems useless or personal.

If you are uncomfortable playing games of your own, or if he carries exactly the car you want, you have a couple of other options. One is simply to ignore him—pretend he isn't there. Another, which can be fun, is to answer his questions with your questions. Keep a question ready for him at all times. The dialogue may go like this:

SELLER: Who is this car going to be for?

BUYER: What size tires does this car use?

SELLER: Where will you be taking your first trip?

BUYER: How big is the radiator?

Ask anything that pops into your head. Questions that he won't be able to answer are the most effective. Employing this technique at a T-O house will insure that you meet the whole staff before you leave. Maybe even the manager.

One of the most important tools in your bag of self-defense is the ability to recognize a climate in which you will be hustled. Immediately walk out. Just leave. You don't need an excuse. You owe nothing to the salesman who hustles you. You owe nothing to the house. You do owe it to yourself to get out of there at once, so do it.

Every attempt will be made to sell you something from that dealer's inventory and to keep you from looking elsewhere. The seller will insist, "You told me you wanted a light blue, midsized, two-door with an automatic, power steering and windows, and that it would have to get 30 miles per gallon on the road. This car fills those requirements perfectly. Yet you're telling me you want to go look at some other makes. You really don't know what you want, do you? You told me you knew exactly what you were looking for, and the car I'm showing you right now is exactly what you described. How are you going to walk away from this deal after I've found you just what you said you wanted? You don't know what you want, do you?"

You will be leaned on, coerced, intimidated, made to feel obligated to buy a car from him after he has spent his time with you. One excellent way to stand firm is to take a friend with you. Someone who can stand back and observe without getting emotionally involved, until it becomes necessary to get emotional in your defense! The salesman won't like it much, but that's his problem. Remember the rules mentioned earlier.

The salesperson will ask about your present car. He can garner valuable information about you by spending a few minutes in "friendly conversation" about the car you are now driving. Throw him another curve, don't tell him you own a car.

If you must tell him something, say you have been riding the bus, borrowing a car, but don't tell him anything about your car. You are not going to trade it in (See Chapter 8, "The Trade-In"), so there is no legitimate reason for him to ask you about it.

If you cannot lie to this person who is so willing to lie to you, then simply tell him that your present car will not be a part of this transaction, so you see no reason to discuss it. He will then give you several plausible sounding reasons that you should discuss it. You will have to tell him that that conversation is closed.

The salesman will ask you questions, the answers to which he will methodically file away to help him gauge your vulnerability. Remember, you are there to look at his merchandise. You ask the questions.

He has no legitimate need to know where you work, how much you earn, whether or not you are married, how long you have lived in the area, or any other personal information. You have come to him to look over his inventory of goods for sale. Just keep it on that level and you will survive.

And what if it's a new car you're after?

First, make sure you have read Chapters 6, 8, and 12 at least once and done the arithmetic.

Next, see if you can find anything in this book which supports the decision to buy a new car. Then, if you still wish to toss several thousand dollars out the window, you can buy a new car with a minimum of brain damage.

First, you still need to determine exactly which

make, model, equipment and color you want. You can approach this selection process in a number of ways. Try out a friend's car similar to the one you want. Try out several nice, fresh, used versions. Rent your prospective choice for a day or two.

If you absolutely must, go to a new-car dealer and test drive the model you want. You will be hustled. You will be pitting your strength and will against that of the highly trained con men (and women) we spoke of earlier. You must keep your guard up at all times, or you will end up buying something you don't want for more than your budget.

2. PRIVATE-PARTY SALES

One way to avoid the hassle of dealer induced trauma, is to buy your car from a private-party. This can be a pleasant experience, mutually beneficial to both seller and buyer. It can also be a real bummer. In the automobile business, all is not as it seems, and that can include every facet of the business, even private-party sales.

Most people who sell their own cars are doing exactly that, selling their own cars. (Maybe even as a result of having read this book). But there are also "curbstoners," who pose as owners selling their own cars. There are so many curbstoners at work that some newspapers keep close tabs on all classified car sales in an effort to weed them out. A computer has no difficulty finding them. Their phone numbers keep coming up again and again.

Curbstoners make a living buying and selling

cars without the benefit of a dealer's license. Although it is probably unfair to the few individuals who try their best to treat their unsuspecting customers fairly, we believe that they are so few in number that it is a safe recommendation to walk away from any transaction in which it becomes clear that you are dealing with a curbstoner.

Many of these shade-tree car dealers obtain their merchandise by buying the not-fit-for-sale trade-ins from legitimate dealers. They will then repair what is absolutely necessary to get the car to run, disguise any other problems to the best of their abilities, clean the car enough to make it presentable, and then advertise it for sale as if it were their own car. They often tell some very creative stories about its history.

While there is nothing at all wrong with an automobile which has been properly repaired (more on this later), there is often a lot wrong with the so-called rebuilt cars being sold by curbstoners who will not be available tomorrow to answer your questions.

Where do the backyard rebuilders get their merchandise? Many auto-salvage dealers make a practice of selling "rebuildables," wrecked cars which have been sold at insurance salvage auctions, and they are often listed as such in newspaper classifieds.

Some of these cars do fall into the hands of competent shop-owners who have the expertise, equipment and desire to do a proper repair job. Many do not. Most questionable rebuilds are easily detected by using the guidelines in "Check It Out."

But how do you identify a curbstoner? First, many are careless enough to have several cars around which appear to belong at the same residence. Ask, "Are any of these other cars yours, too?" If the answer is, "Yes", chances are good that they haven't been his long.

Some curbstoners are more careful and will make a point of removing any other cars so that it appears the one for sale is really his car. One thing to check when you first see the car is the date on the license plate sticker.

If your state issues stickers with the month of expiration, it is easy to tell when the sticker was issued. If it was within the last month or so, keep this information in mind when you listen to the seller's story about how long he has owned the car. Possibly, even though the seller has the title and it is in his name, he registered it for the sole reason of disguising the fact that he only recently acquired the car.

Since almost nobody ever asks these questions, unless he's a real pro, he will by now have grown uneasy enough with your line of questioning that you will be able to see his tension. It may be time to leave. His is not the only car for sale.

If your conversation leads you to believe that you are dealing with a curbstoner, ask him whether or not he has the title to the car. When he says that he does, ask him if it is in his name. If it is not, ask him who owns the car. If he says he does, ask him why the car is not registered to him.

If the transaction progresses to the point where you are shown the title of the car, observe the date that it was issued. Again, if it was in the last month or two, how does this check out with the seller's story of how long he's owned the car? Remember to ask questions, for there is still time to walk away.

Another reason to examine the expiration date on the plates is to be aware of an upcoming renewal fee.

There are also enterprising curbstoners who make a good living by watching the local classified advertising weeklies and being the first in line to call on any car which appears to be priced too low. They buy all of the clearly underpriced cars they can get their hands on, then turn around and re-advertise them at a substantial profit in the regular newspaper Sunday classifieds.

These curbstoners do not buy junk and doctor it up for resale. They rely on their constant attention to market values. They make their profit by taking advantage of the probability that most people looking for a car in the classifieds cannot drop everything moments after the paper hits the newsstand. They can and do, and that's what "entrepreneur" means.

When you find a seller who passes your tests for legitimacy, the only thing left to do is to check out the car itself. That process is covered in detail in Chapters 14 and 15.

There are many distinct advantages in buying a car from its owner, especially from its original owner. The price will usually be less than at a dealership, and most owners will be able to furnish you with a history of the car's performance, maintenance, and repairs. Often the original owner has receipts for everything that has ever been done to his car.

Many people feel that they are safer buying from a dealer because the private-party seller will not guarantee the car. See Chapter 6, "Warranties."

The one-on-one climate, in which many private-party auto sales are conducted, is clearly a pleasure compared to the barrage of abuse bestowed upon anyone entering many dealerships. But even in the more personal climate, you need to be alert for signals which tell you that something is wrong.

Always keep in mind that your appraisal (or that of your mechanic) will decide the fitness of the car. If your appraisal doesn't give you the same message as the sales pitch from the seller, trust your appraisal. Any time a seller refuses to allow you to show the car to your mechanic, try somewhere else.

Of course, you must be reasonable, too. You can't expect a seller to allow you to take the car to a mechanic 20 miles down the road. If you don't have someone nearby to inspect the car, you should take someone along with you to check out any car that you are really serious about.

You can always leave a deposit on a car, effectively making the purchase subject to the approval of your mechanic. Be sure to get a receipt for your refundable deposit.

Even if you feel qualified to do the inspecting yourself, it is not a bad idea to take along a friend when you go car shopping. A capable third party can often find discrepancies that you might overlook.

Avoid telling a seller that what he has to offer is exactly what you want. Even if it is, your bargaining position will be better if you let him know that his isn't the only one around, and you're not that fond of green anyway.

3. THE "BOOK" AND ITS MYSTERY UNRAVELED

Oh yes, and about your trade-in, we can allow you the "book value." Or perhaps you've heard this one, "I'll sell you this fine car at 'low book.' Now, that's what I call a deal!"

What is this bible of the used-car business? The two books you will most often see car dealers flash are the *National Automobile Dealers Association (N.A.D.A.) Official Used-Car Guide* and the *Kelley Blue Book*. Both are known as "the book."

Each is a regional periodical, published regularly as a magazine. There are several editions of each book. Each edition allegedly contains information specific to various regions of the country.

According to the publishers, the information the books contain is obtained from auction reports and dealers' retail sales reports, and is as accurate as possible. Accurate, here, is a subjective term, making the book an interesting phenomenon.

Some novice dealers make big mistakes and lose a lot of money by assuming that the book provides an objective reflection of cars' worth. For the book to be useful, it needs to be interpreted by someone who is on top of current market conditions.

The only way anyone can learn to interpret the book is by careful, continuous, and consistent monitoring of the actual market. Most dealers accomplish this by attending all of the auctions they can make time for, and by reading the market reports published by those auctions. The reports list the cars sold for the week. Some list only a representative sampling of the actual sales. They list year, make, model, miles, equipment, and sometimes a code for condition. Again, the reports need to be interpreted.

Here are some examples of how the book deviates from reality in our own region. At any wholesale auction, any late-model, upper-end Toyota will bring at least $500 more than the book declares is its wholesale value. A really sharp one can bring up to $1,000 over.

Older Chrysler products, particularly "K-cars," will bring somewhere between half of their book to $500 under.

A full-sized, loaded Oldsmobile Brougham four-door will bring its book value if the car is sharp. But the same car in the two-door version will bring about $1,500 less than the book says it's worth. Confusing? You bet.

That the average person buying an occasional car can interpret the book is highly unrealistic. For this reason, it is best to ignore any claims a dealer tries to substantiate with his book.

For example, a buyer might pick an auction report off the dealer's desk and see the car she's been looking for, say a four-year-old Olds Cutlass Supreme, sold for $2,400. She wonders why the dealer told her he would have to pay $6,000 for one when the list says he can buy them for $2,400. But if she had read down the report a little further, she would have seen a same-year Cutlass Supreme that sold for $6,450. And the dealer knew she would not have accepted the $2,400 version.

We have attended auctions with identical-seeming units with nearly the same miles on them. Yet one of these seemingly-identical cars would sell for half the price of the other car. Why? The difference is sometimes obvious, sometimes more elusive. It is primarily the overall condition of the car.

To a dealer who looks at thousands of cars a year, the difference between a fresh, well-maintained car, and a dog which was carefully cleaned up to look like a fresh, well-maintained car, is detectable. The price reflects the difference.

Consider this: you check out a car that wholesales for half its book value. The car shows 60,000 miles and appears to be in good shape. The dealer tells you that he's got that one on special (today only, of course) and it's SO cheap . . . why, he's got it priced at only $100 over wholesale. He shows you the wholesale figure in the book. But at $100 over wholesale book, he's doubling his money if he bought it for half of wholesale book.

Now, you walk over to another three-year-old car and ask him if he'll sell you this one for the same kind of deal. Not much chance if the other model is one that will bring its book value at the auction, meaning that it must retail for far more for the dealer to profit.

Another trick often used to manipulate book figures to the salesman's advantage is to show the high-mileage deductable when appraising a trade-in, or to conceal the high-mile deduction when demonstrating the value of the car he's trying to sell. Or showing you the low-mileage add-on table for the car he's trying to sell, but not showing it when appraising an incoming car.

Examples: the book directs you to deduct a whopping $1,700 from the value of a two year old mid-sized car showing 80,000 miles on the odometer. Conversely, if your five-year-old, mid-sized car has only 35,000 miles on it, you can add $1,000 to its book value. In real life, a sharp five-year-old car with only 35,000 miles on it would likely bring more than just $1,000 over its book (depending, of course, on what kind of car it is).

As a basic rule of thumb, the book values presume 15,000 miles per year to be normal, with anything under or over that amount decreeing either low or high mileage.

The book also gets used for creative financing on occasion, working well with cars that normally sell way below their supposed book value. For example, if you wanted to buy a certain sedan which had a book wholesale value of $4,000, and your bank would finance 75% of wholesale, you could borrow $3,000 on the car.

If you're looking at a car that sells for less than its $4,000 wholesale book value, you could likely buy it even from a dealer, for $3,000. But since the bank won't finance 100% of an auto purchase, the deal gets written up showing that you're paying $4,000 for the car with $1,000 down, and the bank comes up with the "remaining" $3,000. The phantom $1,000 is never paid.

This system works only with those cars which sell for substantially less than their book value, and only at dealerships who will bend a scruple to make a deal.

The bottom line is, do not ever rely soley on the "book" for any information you intend to use in making decisions which can cost you money!!

If you are trying to establish the actual cash value (ACV) of your present car, see Chapter 8, "Trade-ins."

Even bank loan officers, who use the book in their daily decision making, get led astray in both directions; they will loan more on some cars than they are actually worth on the market. Their trusting the book puts both the bank and its customers in a precarious position when they grant auto loans on cars which depreciate faster than the loan gets paid down. Or they will often deny other customers their loans when the book fails to reflect the real value of one of the many cars which consistently sell for more than book price.

In summary, the "book" is not only useless to the occasional autopurchaser, it is misleading and dangerous to rely upon.

4. DEALER AUCTIONS AND SALVAGE POOLS

Everything you ever wanted to know about auctions but didn't know enough to ask. . .

Wholesale dealers' auctions allow licensed auto dealers to buy and sell cars in an environment which excludes the retail public.

In the normal course of business, retail auto dealers acquire vehicles which, for various reasons, they choose not to offer for sale on their own lots. For example, we know one dealer who just hates Nissans. He had one come apart on him once and he spent a bundle on it trying to get it made right. So, now he'll take one in on trade if he can steal it, but it will go to the auction as soon as possible.

Some dealers specialize in certain types of cars, and other trade-ins just don't fit in. The brand X cars go to the auction.

Lease companies use auctions to liquidate their cars when they reach a certain mileage limit. (Some of the best late-model units we've ever bought were ex-lease vehicles.)

Banks and finance companies also use auctions to get rid of their repossessions, which in tough times, come through by the hundreds.

The wholesale dealers' auction is the outlet for these cars. Many dealers rely on auctions to keep their inventory supplied.

Dealers also buy cars which they select expressly to resell at different auctions where they know (or hope) that the cars will bring a higher price. Some dealers, "wholesalers," buy and sell auction-to-auction exclusively. They spend a lot of time getting to know the markets in different parts of the country, for what sells low in southern California might bring a premium in Idaho. The trends change constantly, and for a wholesaler to keep operating at a profit, he must research his market constantly.

Unfortunately, many of the cars offered for sale at auctions are not what they appear to be. Wholesale dealers' auctions are the outlet of choice for slipshod rebuilders and lemon dealers.

Some of the cars that show up at auctions every week are so obviously trashed together wrecks, that it's hard to believe anyone would buy them, especially a professional dealer. But there are enough shaky dealers willing to unload anything they can buy cheap to keep the business brisk.

Where do these dubious autos come from? Well, what do you suppose happens to cars that get wrecked, the ones the insurance companies pay off as "totals"? They go to "salvage pools," and are auctioned off to the highest bidder.

What, exactly, is a "total"?

Used to be, a total was a car whose cost of repair exceeded its value. That definition has broadened somewhat over the years, and in the common vernacular in the car business, a total is any vehicle which for any reason, has been paid off by an insurance company. It need not have been damaged at all.

Consider for a moment a stolen car. A car gets stolen, and if it hasn't been recovered after an interval of time determined by the insurer, the owner gets paid off. He buys another car and forgets the whole thing. But his hot car is still out there somewhere.

Some weeks later, the police find the car, undamaged, in another city 800 miles away. At this point, the insurance company owns the car. They bought it when they paid the owner to replace it. The car is considered a total because the insurer paid it off. What does the insurance company do with the car? In many cases, it sends it to the salvage pool.

There are also many cars at the salvage pools with minor damage; less damage, in dollars, than the insurance company would pay in another instance to have the car repaired. Depending upon the specific case, the insurer will either pay to repair a car, or pay off the insured and sell the damaged car at the salvage pool to help recover expenses. We have seen nearly new cars totaled for as little damage as a fender replacement.

Who pays for this seeming extravagance?

We all do. Any expense that an insurance company incurs raises premiums.

Salvage pool auctions are also closed to the public; only licensed dealers and auto wreckers are invited. Salvage pools are the major source for the cars that are parted out in wrecking yards. They are also the source for rebuilders.

Within 100 miles in this relatively rural area of a sparsely populated state, there are two salvage pools. Each holds a sale every two weeks. At each sale, an average of 250 cars is sold. These cars range from old clunkers to brand new. Some are slightly damaged and quite repairable, and others have been hurt so badly that they are no longer recognizable.

Most of the units which, by any stretch of the imagination (and some rebuilders have pretty elastic imaginations), can be rebuilt, are bought by rebuilders and will appear on the market again, usually at the wholesale auctions. All of the dealer auctions declare that they will not tolerate rebuilds, but our experience has shown us that they do.

Some states have recently enacted legislation making it mandatory for insurance companies to turn in the title of any car they pay off in full, or total, in an effort to ensure that the cars in question will not be rebuilt and sold without disclosing to the buyer that the car had been damaged.

But it is easy to transport wrecks to another state which has no such rules. This is common practice. Truckloads of insurance totals are shipped to different states which allow re-registering the cars with a minimum of hassle. In some states wrecks can be rebuilt and re-licensed as long as the insurance company involved allows it.

For example, on auction day at the salvage pool

in a lenient state, some of the cars will be available to dealers or wreckers, and some will be listed as "wrecker only." The cars listed as wrecker only will be sold without titles; all the others will have clear, marketable titles. Often cars damaged so badly that they could never be rebuilt will be available with titles to dealers or wreckers. And at the same sale there will be other units, some nearly new, with very minor and easily repairable damage, marked "wrecker only." The insurers have decided that these cars have to be parted out.

A car with no title will sell for about half as much to a wrecker who is going to part it out than it would have to a rebuilder. Guess who pays the insurance company's loss? You do.

Although you will probably never attend a salvage pool or a wholesale auto auction, it is to your advantage to know what goes on there. There are decent vehicles at auto auctions. There are also decent dealers who will pay the top dollar prices these cars will bring. We will show you how to find these dealers and how to identify the cars.

Here is one example of how truly excellent cars find their way to dealer auctions. A dealer comes across an exceptional vehicle with low miles which shows all the signs of having had loving care. He doesn't even try to retail it, it goes right to the auction. Why?

He knows his customers don't know the difference between a truly fine car and a well detailed average ride. And he knows that another dealer who has both a sharp eye and a clientele who know the difference will be willing to pay that difference. That's why an extra-sharp car will often go to the auction instead of the retail lot. Here's how that works.

Someone has just had the bad judgment to trade in his six-year-old, loaded Olds Regency Brougham with 19,000 miles on it, on a brand-new Honda Civic, in order to "get better gas mileage." A six-year-old, top-of-the-line Olds with 19K on the clock (as they say) is premium merchandise.

The Honda dealer could put it on his used-car lot at $1,000 over retail book and see what happens. It might sell right away, but the chances are it would not. Most buyers would rather have his other Regency Brougham, the one showing 50K, for $1,000 less money.

But at the dealer auction, there will be hundreds of dealers from all over the home and neighboring states. Of all those dealers, the chances are better than excellent that one of them has a customer waiting for just this car. That dealer, who has a sure sale awaiting him, will pay the price.

When we retailed premium cars, people would often tell us that they "could buy the same car" for a thousand dollars less down the road. We got tired of trying to explain the difference in value between a cream puff and an average car, so we just took our cars to the auction. We have sold premium cars at auctions for $1,000 more than we were asking at retail!

Some of the best buys at dealer auctions are lease returns. These are usually current-year or one-year-old cars, and are generally in top condition. They will usually have from 10 to 25,000 miles on them, and will be available with a wide range of options.

Lease returns bought at auctions often make up the bulk of the inventory on a large new-car store's used-car lot. Many dealers will deny that they ever buy used cars from anyone; all the cars on their used-car lots are trades. Yet, these same dealers are often regulars at the auctions, restocking their inventory.

Again, why? Because of the cars that dealers take in trade, only some are good enough to retail on their lots. If dealers had to rely on trades to keep their lots full, they would be in trouble. Most cars over three years old at the auctions show close to 100,000 miles on them. That's why any vehicle over about three years old that doesn't have a lot of miles on it sells at a real premium.

As we will cover in more detail in Chapter 8 "Trade-ins," it is important to understand that if you trade in your less-than-nice, tired old car with a few dings here and there and bald tires (you're certainly not going to pop for new tires just to trade in the old boat, right?), it will in all probability get sent straight to the auction.

It is also important to understand that since the dealer knows within a few dollars what your old car will bring at the auction, he will not give you more for it in trade than he knows the car will bring.

There are precious few really nice cars at the auctions. This is particularly true with cars more than three or four years old. This is also why wise dealers often take truly nice, low-mileage, older units to the auctions. Since they are likely to be among very few there which don't have more than 80,000 miles on them and are obviously not rebuilt junkers, they get lots of attention, lots of eager bidders, and top dollar prices.

5. THE "FTC" STICKER

A few years ago, the Federal Trade Commission invented a document known to the public as the "Buyers Guide" and to the trade as the "FTC Sticker." It became law that this document be affixed in a conspicuous manner to all used vehicles for sale to the public by dealers. Any violations to this new law are punishable by an immediate $10,000 fine per incident.

So now, when you visit any dealer's lot, you will find a prominently displayed document in the window of each and every vehicle. That document will inform you of either of two things: that the car has no warranty and is being sold as-is, or that the car has a warranty and the terms follow, in finer print, on the document itself.

Government protection, right? Mainly for the dealer. This document does very little for the customer, but does wonders to protect the dealer from customer complaints, no matter how bad the car turns out to be. "FTC" becomes something like "Fool The Customer," for once he signs the FTC sticker, the customer accepts the dealer's terms of sale.

Most dealers now act as agents for insurance companies selling warranties. Most familiar is the warranty which the dealer advertises as "Two Year Parts and Labor Warranty . . . Covers Every Part of the Car . . . Covers Emergency Road Service . . . Rental Car . . ." and then in fine print, "available." This means that for a price, the dealer will sell you an insurance policy which protects you in the event that the car he sells you falls apart. If you elect not to buy this policy, you have no guarantee whatsoever. And when you buy the car, you have to sign the FTC sticker, acknowledging that you are buying the car absolutely "as-is." If the transmission blows up as you leave the lot, it's your problem, and don't expect the dealer to help. This is not much better than a private sale, after all.

The whole thing adds up to more profit to the dealer. Either the customer buys an expensive warranty (read: insurance policy) on which the dealer makes a handsome profit, or he signs an as-is form which effectively assures him no legal recourse even if he was sold a lemon intentionally.

Before the FTC sticker appeared on the scene, you could purchase a car from a reasonable and reputable dealer and safely assume that he was not trying to unload a can of worms on you. If something drastic did happen to that car before you made it a mile down the road, the dealer would usually help. And indeed, that was often the case.

For example, Charlie just signed the papers on a

48

nice-looking, three-year-old car. Ken, Charlie's reasonable dealer, gave him the keys, and he proudly headed home. A few miles from the dealership, there was a loud clang and the rear wheels locked up.

Now Ken had had no idea that the car was going to break. Had he driven it home that day, he would have been no less surprised than Charlie. Fortunately for Charlie, Ken was a dealer who valued his reputation and Charlie's repeat business, and he repaired the car.

"Reasonable" is the operative word here. To too many dealers, the bottom line is more important than repeat business or any kind of good will. Yet there are several ways in which Charlie's case might have been handled.

If he had bought the car at the used-car lot of a new-car dealership, a common approach would be the dealer's offer to fix the car at "his cost," meaning that he will charge Charlie his in-house costs, which have a generous profit margin factored into them. It also means that Charlie could probably have the car repaired at any independent garage for a lot less.

Some dealers might elect to let Charlie return the car, as long as he traded it for another from their inventory. This would get Charlie off the hook for the lemon and would give the dealer a chance to recover the repair costs in the profit on another sale, particularly if he can do some creative selling on the replacement car.

But now that the industry has the wonderful FTC sticker, even a reputable dealer like Ken can, with a clear conscience, tell Charlie, "It's your problem."

After all, if Charlie chooses not to take advantage of the warranty Ken offers (to sell) him, he will have to sign a form saying he agrees that he is buying the car as-is.

Buyers now have no grounds to take dealers to court, because the judge will toss the case out as soon as the dealer presents the as-is clause that the buyer signed.

The exact wording on the FTC sticker is, "You will pay all costs for any repairs. The dealer assumes no responsibility for any repairs regardless of any oral statements [made] about the vehicle." So the dealer can tell you, "Oh, I have to put that form on the car to satisfy the Feds. Not to worry, though, we stand behind every car we sell. Trust me, I'm a dealer."

Then when the car breaks down the day after the sale, the dealer is legally off the hook because you signed the FTC sticker. After all, the form advised you not to listen to the dealer. It said that what he said did not mean a thing. The Federal Trade Commission assumes that the dealer is a liar. And the Federal Trade Commission calls this "consumer protection."

In summary, should you decide on a car being offered by a dealer, unless you can get him to fill in the "warranty" section of the FTC sticker with the details of his own warranty and any verbal promises he made, you have no warranty.

You ought not consider buying a car marked "AS-IS/NO WARRANTY" unless you are prepared to take care of any repairs yourself. If you buy a car as-is, make sure you get a great price on the car or that you are very sure of its satisfactory condition, or better yet, both.

6. WARRANTIES

New-car factory warranties have been improving as manufacturers use them as competitive selling points. Most are limited, meaning that not everything is covered by the manufacturer. What is covered, is covered only under certain conditions.

Coverage varies from one year or 12,000 miles to five years or 50,000 miles or more, and some have no mileage limits. Some offer different terms for different things: 24 months or 24,000 miles on most of the car, five years or 50,000 miles on the drive train, six years or 60,000 miles on body rust-through, as examples. Factory warranties are included in the selling price of the car.

Extended warranties, sold through dealers and backed by outside companies, are essentially insurance policies. The buyer assumes he will have trouble while he owns the car, so he prepays some of the cost of repairs to avoid having to pay more when trouble comes. Cost and terms: exactly what is covered, how, and for how long, determine how good a policy is.

The buyer can keep the odds in his favor by considering the length and depth of the factory coverage, by depending on the good reputation of the car, its manufacturer, the dealer, and the warranty provider, and by his schedule of proper maintenance of the car itself.

The longer the term and more extensive the coverage, the more an extended warranty profits the dealer. The more likely the car is to need repairs, the higher the cost of the coverage. The only way to come out ahead buying an extended warranty is to keep the car for the length of that warranty, and to sustain a major failure. Not a happy thought.

Dealers are eager to offer these warranties because they profit greatly on the sale of each policy. As much as half of the cost of the warranty goes directly into the dealer's pocket. Because most people do not keep cars long enough to benefit from the warranty, is likely the reason insurance companies offer extended warranties so eagerly. If they were not profitable to the insurer, the warranties would not be available.

Consider the last time you bought a used car with relatively few miles on it. Did you have any major problems with it? Probably not. As dealers who have bought, sold, and owned many cars, we can remember only one with a major mechanical problem. We have sold cars to friends, relatives, and their referrals, and have never been informed of a major failure.

Nearly any car which has not been abused and has less than 50,000 miles on it, will run just fine with no problems far longer than most warranties provide, assuming that it receives at least basic maintenance. Certainly, there are exceptions, but they are rare. If you purchase an automobile using the information in this guide, your purchase will not be one of the exceptions.

Buying one of the insurance policies offered by dealers is rarely a good idea. In the first place, these policies are not offered on any units which the dealer doesn't feel pretty sure about. The company for whom the dealer is an agent will terminate the business relationship with any dealer who habitually sells cars which result in claims against the company.

In the second place, the policies are expensive. You would have to suffer a major failure to break even on the price of the policy. Yes, it happens occasionally. But if it happened often enough to make the policy a good value, the policies would not be available. Buying an extended coverage warranty is not unlike dropping a dollar in a slot machine. It may be possible to hit a jackpot, but the casino is not about to lose money.

In all our years in the auto business, we have had one transmission go out on an inventory car, one. Out of 100's and 100's of cars, many with over 100,000 miles, we have had one major problem. The bad transmission was on a Chevy Citation, and had we paid better attention when checking out the car, we wouldn't have had even that one. (In our test drive, we didn't notice that reverse was slipping because we never bothered to back the car up.)

The chances of a major mechanical failure on any late-model car which passes the tests outlined in this book are almost zero.

Many people who could ill afford new cars, have bought them purely because they felt that the warranty they got with that new car was some kind of bullet-proof protection. Over the years, we have listened to many stories of franchised dealer warranty abuses.

Most of them work something like this. Jane bought a new car with a one-year, 24,000 mile warranty. In about two months, and with less than 3,000 miles on the car, she told the dealer that the car seemed to be running too hot. For no apparent reason, it actually boiled over more than once.

The dealer, with his customary warm, friendly smile, signed the car into the service department. After only a week, Jane got it back. She never even asked what was done to correct the problem, she was just happy to get her car back.

At six months, it happened again. The car started to overheat. Coolant boiled out of the radiator. There was steam everywhere. Jane had the car towed back to be repaired. She was certainly relieved that she had the warranty when she thought how all this might have turned out if she had bought the car used.

Jane's car continued to overheat and was taken to the shop until, much to the dealer's relief, her warranty finally ran out. The first time the car overheated out of warranty, the dealer told her that the engine had a bad cylinder head and the replacement would cost her $478.73.

Since she had already had so much trouble with

this car and was now facing a large repair bill, and since he felt really bad about the whole situation, the dealer smiled and offered to make her a really good deal on another new car.

Jane was fed up with the old new car and all of its problems, and since the nice dealer did fix it for her so many times, and was now offering to get her out of this predicament by making her a really good deal on yet another new car, how could she refuse? She did not. Jane traded in her lemon on another new car with a shiny new car warranty.

And what happened to the lemon? Our son (who, yes, should have known better and thus will remain nameless) bought Jane's old new car from the same dealer's used-car lot. The day after he bought it, he and his bride came for a visit. He told us that he had just made a great deal on a used Ford Tempo that ran OK, if a little rough.

We asked him if he had checked for evidence of a blown head gasket, saying that that particular engine had a reputation for bad cylinder heads and blown head gaskets. He went out to look at the engine and his grin disappeared. Sure enough, there was the gungey residue of coolant leaks down the side of the engine. There was also evidence of boiled over coolant all over the engine compartment.

We were a bit disturbed by the fact that a dealer had sold this kid and his wife a car he probably knew was defective. We were wondering what we could do about it since the kids had signed the FTC sticker as-is, when our son found a receipt in the glove box bearing Jane's name and address. We called Jane and she told us the history of the car while she had had it. She had felt all along that she was being taken for a ride, but had not been sure and didn't know what to do about it.

The car's reputation made the failure predictable. The first time Jane brought it in, the dealer had to know that, in all likelihood, the cylinder head would ultimately have to be replaced. He planned from the beginning to put it off until the warranty ran out. Each time Jane came in with the same problem, the dealer did a band-aid repair that he knew would get her down the road a while longer.

As it turned out, not only did he get out of honoring the warranty that Jane thought was her protection, he also managed to make another profitable new car sale out of Jane's dilemma. Then he did yet another band-aid repair on her failing trade-in and unloaded it on another unsuspecting customer.

Because the kids had signed the FTC sticker and did not want to admit having been so foolish in the first place, the dealer got away with his scam on both fronts.

So much for new-car warranties.

So much for buying new cars.

7. INSURANCE

Dealing with insurance companies is just one more way you can get screwed to the wall. But the purpose of this discussion is not to blackball the insurance business; it is only to make you aware of what can occur so that you will have the means to protect yourself. A classic insurance ripoff follows:

Drift back, if you will . . .

It was 1985, and you just bought yourself a shiny, new (shame on you), top-of-the-line Buick with all the toys. Of course, you told your nice insurance man about your new car, and of course you bought full coverage insurance.

When you winced at the rate he quoted you for collision insurance, he patiently explained to you that the reason for the high premium was that the costs of repairing collision damage on a brand new, expensive car like yours were simply astronomical,

57

and that your premium had to reflect these costs. He showed you the cost for your coverage right there on his rate schedule, and that was what you had to pay.

So you paid. Then for the next several years, you paid some more. Each six months, when the renewal came up, you paid it again. The premium even went up once or twice during the last few years, right? But the old Buick was such a wonderful car, you decided when the speedometer logged 100,000 miles that you would just keep it until it would go no more.

Now, let's drift into the future. It is now 1996. One dark night as you are driving home on very icy streets, you lose control and the car skids into a retaining wall. Not hard enough to hurt anyone in the car, but certainly hard enough to pretty much wipe out the front end of the good old Buick.

You call your nice insurance man, the one who has been faithfully renewing your expensive collision policy for the last ten years. He tells you that he will have an adjuster out there in the morning to appraise the damage.

The next morning the adjuster comes out to look at the car, walks around it slowly, shakes his head, and writes on his estimate form, "Cost of repairs exceeds value of car. TOTAL LOSS." He tells you that this old car isn't even in the book any more, but even though it has well over 100,000 miles on it, he will allow you $500.

Your insurance agent never bothered to tell you that it didn't make any sense to pay collision premiums on that old car any more, did he? You just lose your well-maintained, dependable automobile, and the insurance company is going to give you $500 to replace it.

The preceding scenario actually happened. When the Buick became involved in a major accident, the adjuster told the proud owner that since the car was so old, the company was not about to pay to have it fixed like new even though the owner had paid for insurance for years for that very purpose: to repair the car to whatever condition it was in before it was damaged.

Another dirty little scam which some insurance companies are running right now goes like this. If a car is involved in an accident, the adjuster will not allow the repair shop to use new factory parts if there are any cheap forgeries available. These aftermarket imitations include most bolt-on sheet metal, such as fenders, hoods, some doors, bumpers, and a lot of plastic parts, such as headlight moldings and grilles.

The quality control on most aftermarket parts is a joke. Ask any auto body repairman. The fenders don't fit, the character lines don't match, sometimes the installing technician even has to drill new bolt holes because the original ones were all in the wrong places. Hoods are wavy and don't fit up to the fenders. Some hoods are assembled with no welding anywhere; they are so flimsy that they sag four inches when set on the hood prop-rod (the rod designed to hold the hood up from one side or the other).

The corrosion protective primers used on factory parts, which is extra important in any part of the country where roads are salted, is non-existent on the aftermarket replacements. The chrome-plated aftermarket parts look terrible when brand new, and the chrome plating itself is substandard. The plastic parts rarely fit against either factory or other forged parts.

While it might be excusable to use these inferior parts in the repairs of a six- or eight-year-old beater, to expect the owner of a nearly-new car (or an old car that has been carefully maintained) to settle for having his or her car repaired with junk parts is unconscionable. It is particularly unforgivable after the owner has paid a lot of money each year for collision premiums which promise that the car will be properly repaired.

Premiums are supposed to be based upon what it costs to fix the car correctly. Yet usually the insurance company will declare, after a claim is filed, that they will pay only for use of cheap aftermarket parts.

Another area in which insurers often attempt to cut corners is in refinishing collision damage.

Are you familiar with those beautiful, clear-coated glamour finishes available on most newer cars? Well, the only way that these finishes can be properly matched in a repair job is to use a two-stage (sometimes three-stage) system similar to the one with which the car was originally finished. It is necessary that a basecoat of color be applied first, followed with subsequent coats of clear. These materials cost more, and more time is required for the preparation and application of the multi-stage system.

Yet many insurance adjusters simply deny these charges on the shop estimate. They tell the shop that the company will pay only for a standard single-stage paint repair, and that if the insured wants it done right, he will have to pay the difference.

One really unfortunate factor in this is that many car owners don't know the difference. The insurance company dictates to the body shop what they will pay for, the body shop goes ahead and does the job in the half-hearted manner they know they will get compensated for, the insured comes in and looks over the car in the dim light of the shop, decides that it looks OK, and another hatchet job goes out on the street.

Even if a poorly done paint repair looks all right at the time it is accepted, it won't for long. The single-stage paints, particularly in the light metallic shades, do not last as long as the two- or three-stage paint jobs. The insurance companies are clearly cheating their customers out of millions of dollars every year.

Yet another gimmick involves the use of "straightened and rechromed" bumpers. Very few adjusters will allow a shop to replace a damaged bumper with a new one, even though premiums are based upon repair costs using new parts.

These econo-bumpers can be spotted easily on a fresh repair job because they have waves, ripples, grinder marks, and other flaws right on the outside where they are plainly visible. But straightened and rechromed bumpers cost the shop (and the insurance company) about 25% less than new bumpers. Should you inspect the backside of a new bargain bumper, you will likely see the chrome coming off in a number of places.

Why? Steel, in order to have chromium stick to it properly, must be copper plated first. New bumpers are copper-plated. The straightened-and-rechromed-bumper businesses usually omit this step and just plate right over the repair and whatever old chrome is still on the bumper. New straightened and rechromed bumpers often start to rust through in less than a month.

Of course, most newer cars now have plastic bumpers: thin, fragile, super-expensive plastic covers over a metal reinforcement. It is not uncommon for a plastic bumper cover for a mid-size car to cost several hundred dollars. And that's just for the plastic cover. It doesn't include painting the black plastic to match your car, or any of the super-expensive metal structure that supports the cover.

So now insurance companies stipulate that the covers have to be repaired, not replaced, when damaged. It takes a certain amount of skill and craftsmanship to do an acceptable repair on a plastic bumper. In most cases, the repair will be obvious and you, the customer, will just have to live with it.

By allowing use of aftermarket parts only, the insurance company can effectively depreciate the value of your car by hundreds of dollars, sometimes thousands. After repair by their standards, it will look like a rebuilt wreck. But so what? They save a few bucks.

About the only means you have to protect yourself against this common thievery is to insist that your collision policy contain language which spells out clearly that in the event of a claim for repairs on your car, only new, factory parts will be used; and that the shop, not the adjuster, will decide which parts need to be replaced rather than repaired.

Hanging on the office wall in most body shops is a sign which spells out the law that prohibits an insurance company or an agent of that company from telling you where to have your car fixed after an accident. This law is largely ignored by many insurance adjusters and agents. Some insurers even advertise that "their" shops do quality repairs. No wonder so many people can't be convinced that they have the right to decide where their cars will be repaired.

One woman came to us in tears, asking if she really had to take her car to a particular shop with a reputation for terrible repair work. Her insurance agent had intimidated her until she felt that if she tried to take her car elsewhere, the insurance company would not pay the claim at all. We could not convince her otherwise. The agent had done his job well. He had also received his usual kickback from the shop for sending the work there.

Kickbacks and other favors are common between repair shops and insurance people. Want another example?

A two-week-old Flashy Spendymobile just slid off a slippery road damaging the front bumper, right front fender, and door. The car was towed to Archibald's Body Shop.

Archibald looked it over, drooling. He'd been looking for a Spendymobile for a special customer. The damage looked awful but was actually minor: there was no structural damage, only bolt-on parts that needed to be replaced. The car could easily have been repaired as-new.

When Beauregard the adjuster, Archibald's buddy for years, came in to examine the car, Archie told him it was worth $300 to him if the estimate got written up showing the car as a total loss. Since nobody else from the insurance company would look at the car, Beauregard had a free hand writing up the damage report.

He described the damage as far in excess of what it really was. He listed on his report the "salvage value" of the car, which Archibald found an appealing price and eagerly paid. Beauregard got his three bills, Archibald got his car, the owner got a cash settlement for a new car, and all the folks paying enormous premiums picked up the difference.

Every time a deal is made that allows an individual to obtain favors, one person paying off another to get something he's not entitled to, and premiums go up.

If you ever need the services of a body shop, remember that the choice of shops is yours and yours alone. By law, the insurance company and/or its agents and adjusters can not even recommend a shop, much less insist on one.

If the shop you choose writes an estimate of $1,500 and your adjuster tells you that "his" shop will do the job for $500 less, so that's all the insurance company will pay, you do not have to roll over and play dead. In the first place, there is no such thing as "his" shop. Even in the unlikely instance that the agent simply refers to the shop as "his" because of exemplary work at reasonable prices, it's still a good bet to steer away from the shop of his choice. The odds are in favor of there being more to it than that.

You have the option of going to as many shops as you wish for estimates. And if you find that all of the other estimates fall between $1,300 and $1,700, there is a good reason to assume that there is something wrong with the $1,000 bid from your agent's favorite shop. If "his" shop will do the job for a lot less than anyone else will do it for (and give your man a kickback besides), something's wrong. The difference will show up in the quality of the repair job.

If the agent won't accept the lowest bid from the shops you contacted, tell him that you are going to ask the insurance commissioner if what he is doing is legal. If that doesn't get his attention, call your state's insurance commissioner, who is listed in the yellow pages under the "State Offices" listings. Otherwise, the shop gets a job, the agent gets a kickback, and you get taken again.

If your car is damaged to the point that it cannot be driven around to other shops for estimates, fret not. The other shops will come to you. Go to the shop of your choice and tell the in-house estimator where the car is. In most cases, he will be glad to go examine your car and write an estimate. Especially if your car is being stored at the insurance agent's pet shop and you make it clear to your estimator that you wish to get the car out of there.

Many adjusters and agents will use your urgent need for the return of your car as leverage to get their way. Let them know that you don't care how long it takes to resolve the estimate-for-repairs situation even if that's not the case. As soon as an unscrupulous adjuster knows that you are desperate to get your car back, he knows that if he slows things down enough, you will settle for anything he offers.

Sounds pretty grim? It is often worse than it sounds. We are describing here only the up-front, lightweight swindles that are visible to the public. The deeper you dig, the worse it gets.

Contrary to the assertions of many in the insurance business, you do have rights. And there are honest people in the business. Insurance agents, who sell the policies, have to deal with the knowledge that many of the companies they represent rarely deliver what they promise.

Many agents gloss over loopholes which allow the insurer to get out of paying a claim. But others do take great pains in making certain that their clients are aware of all of possible loopholes. Those are the agents you are looking for.

Find an agent who will point out these loopholes to you and make sure your policy states clearly what it pays for.

A step in the right direction is to go to a few body shops in your area and ask which insurance companies will allow the use of new parts and which ones won't. Which insurers will allow the job to be done right, and which ones send out adjusters to chisel away at an estimate until there is nothing left.

Practices vary from place to place, and from company to company. There are insurers and claims adjusters who will treat you fairly in the event of a loss.

8. TRADE-INS

Recently, a very bright young woman named Iris called and said that a friend to whom we had sold several cars recommended that she ask us to find her the very specific car she was looking for. She said her budget was about $6,000.

She mentioned what she had found at various used-car dealers' lots for about $6,000, and that she was also considering buying a new car as well. The new cars were attractive to her because dealers were discounting their left-over last year's models by as much as $2,000, bringing their prices down to about $12,000.

We asked her why, when she had a budget limit of $6,000, she was even considering a new car. She gave a predictable answer: the new-car dealers offered her more for her trade-in.

Let's see if we can find some logic in her answer.

Her present car had an actual cash value (ACV) of about $1,000. That's what the car would bring at wholesale auction, give or take $100. What the car will bring at the wholsesale dealers auction is the actual cash value. The ACV is what the dealer will allow in real dollars, period. Never more, and usually less.

For a dealer to offer $1,500 for a trade-in with an ACV of $1,000, he simply adds $500 to the price of the car he is selling. That is the standard industry practice.

No dealer is going to give you more than ACV for your trade-in. But almost nobody believes it. Over and over and over, we hear the same old story. ". . . I bought it from Whatsizface Motors because he gave me $1,000 more for my old junk than anyone else would."

He did not!!! He gave you ACV and charged you $1,000 more for your new car than he would have if you had not traded in your old car!!!

Find out your car's ACV before you go shopping. How? Go to three or four dealers and ask them what they would pay you for your car. Cash sale. You're moving to Iceland and under no circumstances are you in the market for a car. You need to get rid of the one you have, and what will they give you for it? You can safely figure that the average offer you get for the car in a cash sale is pretty close to its ACV.

Don't be discouraged if you go to a few dealers who say that they won't buy your car at any price; that all of their inventory is composed of trade ins from their new-car store. Just keep trying until you get some real money offers.

When you've gotten at least three cash offers, the average of these will be close to the ACV of your car. The reason for going to several dealers is that almost every dealer has both favorites and cars he doesn't like. If yours falls into either category, you won't get an objective figure. Especially if it's one he doesn't like.

And once you know the actual cash value of your car, do the sensible thing and sell your car yourself. Run an ad in the paper. Price it at a figure half-way between what the dealers offered and what the same year and model units are advertised for in the classifieds.

If it feels like too much trouble, and you think you just have to trade it in, before you run down to Auto Row, consider this. What if you ran an ad, talked to a half dozen tire-kickers, and finally sold the car for $300 or $400 more than the dealers offered you for it? How long did it take you to do all that? A couple hours? Even if it took three or four hours, $100 an hour probably doesn't compare poorly to what the ol' boss is paying these days, does it?

You are always in a better position to deal if you do not have a trade-in. You are at a distinct disadvantage if you need to trade in your old car to buy the new one. The trade-in is one of most powerful tools in your dealer's customer manipulation bag. If you have a trade, the dealer has the upper hand as soon as you walk in the door, and he'll likely keep it.

New cars, particularly those with optional extras, have a lot more "spread" to work with than do most used-cars. The greater the spread, the greater the opportunity to offer "more" on the trade-in.

If you're not convinced, and you're still going to

trade it in, remember, no dealer is going to give you more than ACV for your car. If he says he will, he's just adding the difference between ACV and his offer to the price of the car he's selling. That's the truth, the whole truth, and nothing but the truth.

If you go into a car purchase with a trade-in, you will lose. Not only will you lose a significant amount over what you can sell the car for yourself, but you will weaken your bargaining position with the dealer. And perhaps most important, you will give the dealer, who is professionally trained to manipulate financial transactions, the winning hand right from the start.

Never involve your present car in the purchase of a new one.

9. FINANCING

I f you look to this chapter for instructions to buy the most car with the least down, you will be disappointed. Ideally you should pay cash for your car. You should save enough money beforehand and then buy a car which you can afford, thereby eliminating interest as an expense of car ownership. But since paying cash is often impossible, if not unAmerican, you may have to find some kind of reasonable financing.

About the only way to buy a car with borrowed money without losing in the process is to buy a special interest car which will appreciate in value over the years. For the rest of us who just want to buy a regular, garden variety, late-model car, drive it until we either tire of it or wear it out (not likely), the first and most important rule of thumb is: Never borrow so much of the price of the car that its value will depreciate faster than the loan gets paid down.

There is a popular scam (one among many) to lure people into new-car showrooms. It allows you to make a tiny, say $100, down-payment, and to make only half-payments for the first year of a five-year contract. As of the thirteenth month, the full payments commence.

The deal sounds great to a lot of optimists who figure they probably won't keep the car for more than about a year anyway, to dreamers who are counting on a sizable raise; it seems a lifesaver to those young couples who can never seem to save up a down payment.

What no one stops to figure out is that those half-payments often don't even pay the interest on the loan, much less any principal. At the end of one year, they could well owe more on the car than they had originally paid for it!

If at the end of the first year (or after a few months of making the now double payments on the now no-longer-new-and-exciting car) the optimists decide that they would like to be relieved of their burden, they will find out that there is no way out of their predicament. The car has depreciated down to $2,000 less than they owe on it.

They now realize what they've gotten themselves into. Their options? Make another four years of payments. Or sell the car and get a personal loan for the $2,000 difference between what they can get for it and what they owe on it. Then they get to pay off the $2,000 for a car they don't even have any more. Or they can allow the car to be repossessed.

If they choose repossession, they will be sued for the difference between what the lending institution sells the car for (often less than it's worth) and the outstanding balance on the loan. At the very least, they'll have a tough time ever getting another loan.

Banks generally won't loan more than about 75% of the wholesale book value of a used car. This way, they are in a reasonably safe financial position if they need to repossess the car. Of course, some cars aren't worth even 75% of their wholesale book value (See Chapter 3), leaving the lending bank in a precarious position.

The single most important point we can make regarding financing of cars is this: Secure your own financing! Under no circumstances should you ever discuss financing with a dealer.

In the first place, the dealer makes a profit from your transaction with the lender, meaning that you could get the financing cheaper elsewhere.

In the second and more significant place, allowing the dealer to bring financing into the transaction gives him the opportunity for more manipulations, and he is thoroughly trained in the fine art of the manipulation of figures. It is in the juggling of financing figures that many buyers pay up to thousands of dollars more for a car than was implied verbally by the dealer. Unless you are skilled in math, some of these manipulations are very difficult to detect.

Always be prepared to pay cash for your car, regardless of where you get the money. Arrange your financing beforehand.

Many people don't know that it is possible to get a financing commitment from their banks or credit unions before they even select a car. Actually, most lenders would prefer that you come to them before you go shopping. That way you can discuss things like credit limits, repayment schedules and interest rates at your leisure, instead of after the car has been chosen, when bad judgment under pressure is more likely.

Tell your lender that you will be buying a car, about how much you plan to budget for the purchase, and how much of that you need to borrow. Ask for a commitment for that amount, so that when you go shopping you will be able to deal for a cash sale, putting you in position for a more favorable transaction.

If you have lending options, such as several banks or a credit union, ask for the interest rate from each. They do vary. Many lenders will offer a lower interest rate on a new-car purchase than for a used car. Forget it! Factor in the incredible instant depreciation of new cars while you try to figure out how much interest you would save. (See Chapter 12.)

Dealers will often advertise unusually low interest rates, especially on new cars. These ads usually also contain language in fine print, spelling out the fact that you can get either the low interest rate or the rebate, but not both. (Did you ever wonder where the rebate comes from?)

Dealers often offer new-car financing interest at rates below those that a bank will allow on a used-car purchase.

Remember Iris in Chapter 8? The $12,000 price tag attracted her because the interest rate was only 9%, as opposed to the 12% she would have to pay at her bank if she bought the $6,000 used-car.

She was going to use her old car as the whole down payment, so she'd be financing $5,000 on the used car, or $10,000 on the new one, since they were going to give her "$2,000!" for her clunker (the one that's actually worth $1,000), on the new ride. The used car, at 12% on a 36-month note would cost about $978 in interest with the payments at $166/month.

The new car, financed for 48 months at 9%, would cost $1,944 in interest, the monthly payments would be $249. Stretched out to 60 months, the payments would drop to $208/month, but the interest would climb to $2,455 over the life of the contract. The used car would end up costing her a total of $6,978; the new one, $13,944 on the shorter of the two contracts.

If she lives in a state which charges 6% sales tax, she can add another $360 to the used car, or $777 to the new one. Many states charge license fees based upon the selling price or book value of the car, making yet another penalty for buying the more expensive unit. And that doesn't include the much steeper insurance premiums for the newer car.

To someone who had decided rationally to stay within a $6,000 budget, the new car should never have been a consideration.

The used car, a week after purchase, is still worth its purchase price. The new car, which is a used car as soon as she signs the papers, will be worth, if she's lucky, $3,000 less than its purchase price. If she adds that $3,000 in depreciation to the greater interest cost of the cheaper-to-finance new car, "cheaper" loses much of its meaning.

10. DECIDING WHAT YOU NEED

There are many factors, some not so obvious, involved in the decision to buy a car. For example, we recently bought a car for our 80 year-old mother, who still drives well. We tried to talk her into a two-door model, since we figured she would have less fussing with two doors. She pointed out that the doors on two-door cars are heavier and harder to open, especially when the car is parked on a slope, and that the longer doors would not open wide in her narrow garage. We bought her a four-door.

If you don't already know what your next auto purchase will be, here are some valuable points to ponder. Consider your family's needs in deciding the number of seats and doors your new car must have. Do you want a coupe, sedan, or station wagon? How about a mini-van or a convertible?

Wagons, all other things being equal, usually cost

more than comparable sedans. New ones cost more to begin with and there are fewer wagons manufactured in any given model year; supply and demand keep the price of wagons higher.

Wagons have more space. But they have the disadvantage of leaving your cargo in plain sight of passersby. In plain sight includes in plain hearing: if your cargo rattles, you have to endure the noise. To some, noise is very annoying. Wagons, especially smaller wagons, also transmit more road noise into the passenger compartment than do sedans.

Another factor is handling. Because of their higher weight aft, wagons generally do not handle as well as other body styles of the same model.

You know those wagons with the flashy wood-grain-looking sides? Unless you are either buying a new car (shame on you!) or find one with the wood-grain decals in primo condition and you plan not to keep the car for more than a couple years, you might want to consider avoiding the wood-grain look.

The wood-grain sides are vinyl sheets not unlike dime-store self-stick shelf paper; and to date, nobody has been able to produce any that will hold up in direct sunlight. Check out the wood-grain sides on any car that's a few years old.

Should you ever damage a panel on your wood-grain sided wagon, you will be in for a hefty bill to repair it. The similarity to dime-store shelf-paper ceases abruptly at the cash register. The same goes for any of the stripe packages found on many of the sportier cars.

There are many new and late-model "sporty" (small and flashy) cars available which get billed by their makers, both foreign and domestic, as "sports cars." In our opinion, it takes more than a few yards of racing stripes and flashy decals to make a sports car.

In an attempt to avoid the endless controversy about what is and what is not a sports car, let's just call all of those sporty little domestic and foreign numbers "personal" cars. The genuine older sports cars, Triumphs, Jaguars, MG's and the like, can still be found. But if one of those is what you really want, you had better either be a mechanic or own one.

The discussions in this book apply to almost any car on the road, but here are some esoteric asides for exotic cars. If you are entertaining thoughts about buying, for example, a Jaguar, and you are not already intimate with these creatures, have someone who knows them well go over your prospective purchase with a fine tooth comb.

One way to be fairly sure that you will find the car's every flaw is to take it to either a Jaguar dealer or an independent who specializes in the marque and who has a service department. Pay his $20 or so fee to inspect the car you're interested in. If he also sells used Jags, it will be to his distinct advantage to find every defect possible so that he can sell you one of his cars.

One more thing to remember in considering body styles is that the flashy, sport-coupe models cost more to insure. Your banker or insurance agent has a copy of the tables which give comparisons of insurance premium costs.

Some cars are more costly to repair than others. Insurers' studies analyze repair cost comparisons of specific types of collision damage. Then they base their code on statistics which show that people who drive those sexy little sports models crash more.

Insurance premiums are also higher on anything which can be called "high performance." The bigger the engine, the higher the premium. This applies to a high-performance image, even if the car is a dog. For example, a plain-Jane Camaro with a V8 engine will often be a "lower risk" than the same year Camaro with a flashy paint job and a name like "Rallye Sport," even if the Rallye Sport has a four-cylinder engine.

Insurance companies thrive on statistics. Yet just how valuable are these magical numbers? Consider this: if you had one foot in boiling water and the other packed in dry ice, you would be statistically comfortable.

How big a car should you get? The popular reason for thinking small is the generalization that all small cars get better mileage than all big ones. But in the real world, some full-size cars will go as far on a gallon of gas as some small ones. Putting a priority on gas mileage alone can be a big mistake, particularly if you have to pay more money for a gas miser than for a bigger car. Yet this is a common rationalization for buying a new car.

Many years ago, when a new VW cost $1,695, it might have been conceivable to make car payments out of the money saved on gas. But many of today's mid- and full-size cars get such good mileage that it would be difficult to justify buying a new $10-20,000 car to "save money on gas."

If you have any interest in remaining rational about this decision, figure it out; the arithmetic is pretty basic and in Chapter 11.

A more realistic parameter to use in deciding car

size is the size of the people and their comfort. If you're six-foot five, most of the compacts and probably all of the sub-compacts are going to cramp your body if not your style.

If you do most of the driving, are four-foot-eight, and your spouse is six-foot-five, you have a different problem. For families with two drivers of dissimilar sizes, a mid-size car with individual seats or a split bench seat is an attractive choice. A tilt-wheel makes the drivers' diverse accommodations even more flexible.

Another option for a tall driver to consider is power windows. Ask any long-legged driver about the knee/window-crank controversy. The power window option eliminates the crank, and restores some precious space for the driver, especially in small cars.

Seats vary a great deal from car to car. Even within different models of the same make, there are a variety of seat configurations. Surprising that after years of perfecting the motorcar, there has been no consensus on an acceptable seat design.

It is a good idea to spend more time than a limited test drive will allow to get the feel of the seats in your prospective new car. On long trips, a driver's seat with adjustable lumbar support and backrest angle can't be beat. The driver's comfort is, of course, more important for the person who often drives long distances than for one who rarely goes farther than a short commute.

Comfort is also more relevant for folks whose backs are less tolerant of the consequences of strained sitting for long periods. If most of your driving is on the open road and you have a family to transport, a full-sized cruiser might be your best bet, especially one which is a few years old but still in excellent condition. Many full-sized cars depreciate much faster than smaller ones, so an older full-sized car may have been largely depreciated when you buy it used.

How risky is it to buy a car with lots of miles on it? This topic comes up in several discussions in this book because it is so widely accepted that lots of miles means worn out. Not true! It is possible to find two identical cars, one with 40,000 miles on it and the other with 100,000 miles, and have the high-miler be in far better shape. We have seen as many high-milers in excellent shape as low-mileage units that were not worth having at any price. There are real bargains available in well-maintained, high-mileage cars.

We recently had in our inventory two apparently identical cars. They were the same make, model and year, had the same colors inside and out, and included the same equipment. Their appearances suggested that they were both in near perfect condition. But one car had 80,000 miles on the odometer and the other had 40,000.

The high-miler had been meticulously maintained and serviced all its life, and the miles were obviously mostly highway. It ran and drove as new. But the low mileage unit had evidently never seen any service at all. It still had the original oil filter on it and, until we changed it, what appeared to be the original oil. The engine was noisy, as was just about everything else mechanical in the car. It did not drive well at all.

Yet when both cars went to the auction, the low-miler sold for $2,000 more than the high-miler. Why? Because dealers know how important the odometer reading is to most buyers.

The key to the worth of a high-miler is in the kind of use and the quality of service the car received over its life. The kind of use includes both the manner in which the car was driven and the kinds of roads it was driven on. Some cars never see a highway and are used for short run, stop and go driving exclusively. That's really hard on a car, and any car being used for short runs needs more frequent service than the manufacturer's recommended schedule provides for. But they rarely get it.

We recently drove an amazingly loose Chevy Citation with only 20,000 miles on it. It rattled everywhere even on fairly smooth roads, and its rough-running engine was way too noisy. The car had belonged to a woman who lived on a ranch in eastern Oregon. It had been her job to deliver lunches to the men working out in the fields, and she used the Citation for those deliveries.

Her car appeared never to have been serviced. It had the original oil filter (and oil?) in the engine. There was no filter element in the dust packed air cleaner. The air cleaner element had apparently become so clogged with dust that it had been discarded and never replaced.

Compared to another of the same make, model and year which has been used primarily on long highway trips, and has been properly serviced at regular intervals for 100,000 miles, which is the better car?

A smart shopper needs to check closely because a

professional detail and service job can make a car like the Chevy Citation just discussed appear to be in good shape.

Don't let an odometer sell you the car. Don't even trust the odometer in the first place. Although recent laws have deterred most shaky dealers from "spinning speedos," it hasn't stopped them all. And the worst culprits are actually not the dealers, but the private parties from whom the dealers get the cars.

There are a lot of people who feel that since most dealers are crooked anyway, what's the harm in beating them at their own game by selling or trading in a car with an "adjusted" odometer reading? Also, up until a few years ago, most cars had odometers which only read up to 99,999 miles. Many times cars with 30,000 or 40,000 miles on the odometer are sold as showing true mileage when in fact the meter has already rolled over once.

We have seen many cars at the auctions showing 20,000, 30,000, or 40,000 miles and looking for all the world like the miles were right, only to hear them announced as "miles over" when they went through the sale. Finding out the truth may take very careful examination.

If the procedures outlined in Chapters 14 and 15 on checking cars out still leave you guessing when examining a car you suspect is "miles over," consult your competent mechanic for a diagnosis. Sometimes the only way to tell is by carefully listening to the engine. A trained ear can usually hear the difference.

If nothing else, this discussion should tell you that a high-mileage car is not necessarily a worn out car. Lots of cars with over 100,000 miles on them are good for at least another 50,000 miles before needing any major repairs.

The good news is that since most people truly believe the high-miles equals worn out myth, these high-mile cars can usually be bought so cheaply that even if you do have to do a major repair in a year or two, you're still way ahead.

We have sold a number of carefully selected high-milers to friends who trusted us and believed what we have just told you, and we've received back nothing but glowing reports of appreciation for the bargains. Not once has anyone to whom we sold a high-miler come back to say it was a mistake.

High-milers up to about three years old represent the most dramatic dollar savers. And let's face it, a two-year-old car with 90,000 miles on the odometer can't have seen a lot of city driving. Straight, constant speed, highway miles just don't wear out a car very fast.

For example, a salesman drives from San Francisco to L.A. During that 400 mile trip, the transmission has to shift through the gears (which is what eventually wears out any transmission) about as many times as does someone driving five miles across town to go shopping. We use the transmission as an obvious example, but there are literally hundreds of wearing parts in any vehicle, and the most wear is produced in the process of stop and go driving.

This is exactly why a late-model, super clean high-miler is generally an excellent choice. It's a pretty safe bet that any car which has logged 30,000 or more miles per year has seen highway miles almost exclusively. Such cars are often offered for sale by the companies whose own employees have logged the miles, in which case, service records are usually available, too. Check your classifieds for late-model cars listed as having high miles.

And remember, if you are looking for an older car, use the same parameters that you apply to a newer one. The only exception is that you have to be more careful in checking out the condition of an older car because the miles will have been logged over a longer period of time.

One more high-miler tip and we'll move on. In sparsely populated parts of the country, a much higher percentage of the available used cars will be all highway high-milers. This is simply because it is often a long way to anywhere in rural areas.

When two cars about the same age, mileage, and condition go through the auction, if one is a deluxe, loaded huge-mobile, and the other is a little econo-car, the econo-car will often bring more money. The older they get, the more significant the difference. One rather silly reason for this is that it is simply not stylish to drive big cars any more, particularly not big, old cars.

The fuel-mileage question comes up again when discussing the big car. How many miles per year do you drive? The "average" person drives 15,000 miles a year. Since it isn't difficult to find a full-sized car capable of 20 miles per gallon, let's use that figure for a comparison.

15,000 miles at 20 mpg consumes 750 gallons of gas. An "average" compact car might get 30 mpg; but let's use a sub-compact that gets 35 mpg for our figuring. 15,000 miles at 35 mpg would use 429 gallons. That's a savings of 321 gallons for the year, or 27 gallons per month. Hardly a car payment, right?

Of course, there are other expenses which can be higher in a bigger car, too; notably collision insurance, tune-ups and tires. However, collision insurance for an older big car will likely be a lot less than for a newer small car. And if your bigger old car is more than about six years old, you might be wiser to buy no collision insurance at all. (Did you read Chapter 7?)

Tune-ups, while they usually cost more for a V8 than for a four-banger, tend to be needed less frequently on bigger cars, especially anything more than about four years old. It is often less expensive to tune-up a simple, easy-to-work-on older car than it is one of the high-tech, ultra-complex, computer controlled new ones.

Tires will cost more for a bigger car and there's no way around that. You will need to do some more arithmetic to decide if the extra comfort is worth the price.

If your figures show that the extra cost of operating the big car is more than you feel is reasonable, there is still a way to have your proverbial cake and eat it, too. Find a nice, big, comfortable cruiser with all the toys, even a few years older than you'd been considering. There were some exceptionally fine cars built in the seventies, and a lot of them are still far from worn out.

Even at a premium price, a 15 year-old car in superb condition will cost a fraction of the price of a five-year-old car in just about any condition. A 15 year-old car also has other distinct benefits. Cars were simpler then and any competent mechanic could service them. Many late-model cars cannot be properly serviced by anyone lacking the correct, incredibly expensive, dedicated, often dealer-only, electronic diagnostic equipment. Not so with the 15 year-old auto.

Most older cars have reputations for super dependability. If you ever bend a fender, a used one for the older car can be replaced inexpensively, not likely with a newer one. And because it is currently unfashionable to drive a big car, even the exceptional ones can be bought for bargain prices. (See Chapter 12.)

The happy compromise, which is evident by its popularity, is the mid-sized car. Over-sixfooters find lots of legroom in cars like GM's Olds Ciera, Chev Celebrity, Pontiac J-6000, and Buick Century, from about 1982 and up. These cars, which are mechanically identical, have earned an enviable reputation: with reasonable care and maintenance, these cars will run well over 100,000 miles with few problems. They perform well and do it all at nearly 30 mpg.

Ford's little LTD and Mercury's little Marquis from the middle- to late-eighties (again, mechanically identical cars) also qualify here, although their gas mileage is not as good as that of the GM mid-size cars.

The only visible concession lost by these cars to their full-size counterparts is in room to stretch. There's plenty of room for the business of driving, though. There are other differences, not so visible, which are extremely important to some drivers. One difference is ride. There is no comparison between the ride and handling of a Celebrity and a Caprice, or between Ford Motor Company's full-size and mid-size cars.

And if safety is one of the more important criteria in your selection of a car, there are several things to consider. Obviously, bigger, heavier cars are safer in collisions than little, lightweight ones; but if you feel safer driving a smaller car, you will likely be safer.

In the quest for the best fuel economy, most small cars are light in all areas: body sheet-metal, as well as the sheet-metal sections which serve as frames and structural inner panels. The suspension components are also as light as possible, and many will give way in a fairly minor accident.

In most mini-cars, it is not uncommon to bend a tie-rod or a strut in even a careless encounter with a curb. In a collision with a full-sized, ten-year-old Buick, a new Toyota Corolla will not fare well.

All other factors being equal, the limited space inside a compact car generally makes it less safe in a collision than a larger car. Your knees, for example, have a much better chance of survival in a front-end collision if they are not already two inches from the dashboard before the accident. The same goes for heads and windshields. Of course, this discussion presumes that you wouldn't even think about driving a car without buckling your seat belt.

We have seen many hundreds of wrecked cars over the years. In serious collisions, none seem to fare enough better than others to make the alleged strength of the body a valid criterion for the selection of one model over another. Big over little, yes; but not one big car over another big car nor one little car over another.

If you are serious about preserving the integrity of the passenger compartment of your car in an accident, buy a full-sized sedan with a heavy door post in the middle, not a hardtop.

The new mini-vans, which have become very popular as family-haulers, have been exempted from many federal safety standards to which passenger cars must adhere, for the vans are classed as trucks. The most notable of these exemptions concerns the use of energy-absorbing bumpers. Although the mini-vans appear to have the same type of bumpers as most other passenger cars, they do not.

Like some of the imported similarly exempt four-wheel drive autos, they have a thin, fragile, plastic cover stretched over a thin, fragile, so-called reinforcement which is made of a lightweight piece of metal that you could dent with a good swift kick of your Nikes. Buyer beware: all is not as it seems to be.

(There is at least one automaker who likes to demonstrate the strength of his cars with ads showing about ten cars stacked one atop the other, and the one on the bottom doesn't even seem to care. Its tires aren't even flat.)

If you are not familiar with the difference and you already know that you don't want a big car, we recommend that you never drive one. You just might find the quiet luxury of a full-size car irresistible. Never mind that lots of '85 and newer full-sized cars are capable of gas mileage in the mid-twenties.

And there are other, more subtle, differences. The use of plastics for finish trim is more evident in the mid-sized cars. Bigger cars, especially the top-of-the-line models, are just plain plush in ways the smaller cars only imitate with plastic.

But if good looks and better gas mileage are what

you need, a mid-sized domestic car might be for you.

How about all those wonderful imports, you say? Well, there are those who would burn this book if we said that imports were acceptable. But a lot of the parts in your Chevy are, in fact, imported. The nuts and bolts that hold the All-American Buick together are metric. (Some mechanics who work on these cars every day haven't yet figured out why their wrenches don't fit quite like they used to.)

When you buy parts for your American car, read the "Made in ..." tags on them. Just about every country in the world is represented on parts tags for American cars.

But we're getting sidetracked. This ought to be good for a few burned books: In our many years' experience owning and operating various auto businesses, not to mention autos, we have found that the Japanese cars since the mid-seventies represent the highest level of craftsmanship, engineering, integrity, and overall quality of any cars made anywhere in the world, not a happy admission.

For example, our shop recently had the door on a nearly-new Cadillac Brougham apart to service a faulty power window mechanism. On this almost new, very expensive car, absolutely no effort had been made to protect anything inside the door from corrosion. Every metal part, including the screws and rivets which held them together, was already covered with a film of rust.

The entire interior of the door was bare metal: no paint, no rust inhibitor. Most of the parts were merely riveted together, demonstrating serious throw-away implications. The door trim panel was attached to the door itself with sheetmetal screws driven right into the metal and several of them had been stripped in the factory installation and quietly hidden where the consumer never looks.

This carelessly manufactured car was not an aging Vega, but a new Cadillac.

The same inner door inspection on a bottom-of-the-line Japanese car would reveal a door shell carefully painted on the inside to protect everything from corrosion, and assembled with cadmium-plated parts and fasteners. Where trim parts attach to the door, nylon grommets are installed to receive the plated attachment screws so that even repeated installations will not strip them out.

Other examples are evident everywhere; sloppy assembly is something you can find on almost any domestic car.

How about the European autos, like Audi, BMW, and Peugeot, for example? Our advice on these is basically to ask the person who owns one, particularly one a few years old. Few owners of brand-new cars will have experienced any significant problems characteristic of the marque, so take your poll from the owners of at least several cars like the one you are considering. Many times, a dealership service manager will tell you about particular years or models of a certain make to look for or to stay away from.

Test-drive a few representative used cars, preferably with 50,000 or more miles showing on the odometer. If you find that out of ten Audis, for example, the power sunroofs didn't work on eight of them, you may consider this flaw typical, and look for a car without that option.

Any European car will be expensive to service and to buy parts for. In addition, parts availability is often limited, meaning lengthy down-times for broken cars.

Since there are significantly fewer dealers for these cars than for domestics or Japanese makes, your sources of parts will be few and far between, and usually only in bigger cities. (See Chapter 17.)

No discussion on determining your needs would be complete without considering engine options. There is a myth afloat that the tiniest engine will deliver the best fuel mileage. And if you want to get a little more technical, there is a similar myth about high rear axle ratios and better mileage, as well. It isn't that simple.

There are many factors which come into play when making these assessments. If you have decided on a particular make and model of auto that offers more than one engine option, ask several service technicians for recommendations. If, as often happens, you find you get a unanimous opinion about a certain engine to stay away from, do so!

In most vehicles used in normal driving, the smallest engine will not yield the best fuel mileage because the small engine has to work so much harder. This is particularly noticeable in pickups, vans and other utility vehicles.

A full-sized pickup with a little six-cylinder engine has to be driven at nearly full throttle to pull the same load up the same hill that a V8 would do with ease. The six will burn more fuel at nearly full throttle than the V8 will while it is loafing. The same goes for passenger cars, only the difference is not usually as dramatic.

Another thing to consider is that an under-powered engine which has to work at nearly its limit most of the time will wear out long before the bigger engine will.

We have had several friends who replaced smallish engines in their motor homes with the biggest engine which would bolt directly into the chassis. They discovered that their rigs not only performed far better, but did so on less fuel.

The same philosophy holds true for axle ratios. Having the option to select an axle ratio doesn't usually apply in used car purchases, but given the choice, the engine size and type of driving must be considered in the decision. As with the under-powered engine, selecting too high an axle ratio will make the engine work harder under any given load, and again, fuel mileage and engine life will suffer.

Generally, given the choice of four-cylinder or V6 engines in the small and mid-sized cars, the V6 is the better bet. They are in almost all cases quieter, smoother-running, longer-lasting, better-performing, and they get about the same overall mileage. If resale value is important to you, the V6 is the only way to go.

Again generally, and there are exceptions which your mechanic will be happy to point out to you, pickups and other utility vehicles do best with middle-of-the-road engines. The muscle engines are overkill and often get lousy mileage, and the little engines are notoriously underpowered.

It is always a good idea to ask around to determine if there is a particular engine which has been proven to be a can of worms. We see, again and again, people buying vehicles with particular engines which are fairly famous for never-ending problems. They never asked, and someone got to unload yet another lemon.

What about options such as power steering and brakes, automatic transmissions, tilt wheel, cruise control, power windows, door locks, seats and mirrors (yes, power mirrors), split bench seats, rear defrosters, exotic stereo systems, and of course, air-conditioning? Let's take them one at a time.

POWER STEERING. On anything bigger than a compact, power steering is more a necessity than an option. Even on many compacts, it is a valuable option if you do a lot of in-city maneuvering and parking. Power steering units have evolved with such dependability that problems are practically unheard of.

Years ago, people used to tell stories about power steering robbing the engine of five or more horsepower, thus causing a noticeable drop in fuel mileage. This is not true. The only time that the power steering pump is doing any work at all is when the steering wheel is actually being turned. Even then, the amount of work it does is directly proportional to the force applied to the steering wheel.

In other words, if you turn the wheel quickly from side to side while your car is parked, the pump is working at its maximum for that movement. If you make a long, sweeping turn on the highway, the pump doesn't do a thing. While you are motoring down a long, straight freeway, the pump is merely along for the ride.

Consequently, power steering is a valuable, dependable, nearly maintenance-free option whose value doesn't depreciate at resale time. As a matter of fact, any non-power-steering car bigger than a sub-compact that comes up for sale at the auctions is considered, as they say in the business, "sale-proof."

POWER BRAKES. Since most cars have been equipped with front disc brakes for quite a few years now, and most disc brake setups require the use of brake boosters, power brakes have been standard on most cars for years. They are listed as a "no cost option" in many cases, but you couldn't order the car without power brakes if you wanted to.

AUTOMATIC TRANSMISSION. Most automatics are extremely reliable, often still performing like new after well over 100,000 miles. On many new cars, they are expensive options.

Since the majority of cars bigger than compacts sold in the last few years have been equipped with automatics, used cars with standard shifts are difficult to find except in a compact or an import not classed as a luxury model. Even some imported "luxury" models have five speeds. All other factors being equal, an automatic transmission adds several hundred dollars to the book value of a car less than four years old. The book presumes that most cars have automatics, and deducts for a standard shift rather than adding for the automatic. If you are looking for a standard-shift car and find one you like, don't tell the seller. Stick shifts are harder to sell: a bargaining point in the buyer's favor.

Assuming that the automatic transmission will last the life of the car, you could justify the initial extra expense by never needing to replace a worn-out clutch. The average clutch can be expected to last about 70,000 miles. If most of your driving is in the San Francisco hills, figure 40,000 or less, depending on your driving skill.

Of course, if you only commute on freeways 50 miles each way every day, you may never wear out a clutch. But if you do, you can count on spending from $200 to $400 to overhaul a worn-out clutch.

From a purely practical standpoint, if most of your driving is in the city, why bother with a gear-shift, especially in an area calling for stop and go driving on steep hills? On the other hand, if you rarely drive downtown, you could probably expect to save a little fuel with a five-speed.

There are some rational pros and cons to both automatic and manual transmissions, but it boils down to a matter of personal choice. Some folks just like to shift gears.

TILT WHEEL. If two drivers of disparate sizes share the car, a tilt wheel may be an extra cost necessity. The tilt wheel, along with an adjustable seat back, is especially nice for varying your driving position on long rides. These comfort extras can be real life-savers for the handicapped, people with back problems, and anyone of unusual proportions.

CRUISE CONTROL. Again, a wonderful strain-saver for long trips. It frees your right foot to move around, thus lessening driver fatigue. Cruise control also does a better job of holding a steady throttle setting than most feet do, resulting in a slight increase in mileage.

Another of its virtues is the elimination of IFS (itchy-foot syndrome). Just set the cruise to the speed of ambient traffic and go with the flow. Cruise control helps you avoid peeking around every bend in the road to see when you could pass the guy in front of you who is going only two mph less than the posted speed limit.

The first cruise control we ever owned was in a big, comfortable Oldsmobile we used to make the same 100 mile, all-highway drive to the auction every week. We were conscientious about maintaining the speed limit, but when riding along in a big, quiet car with the stereo playing, the speed always started creeping up on us.

After the second speeding ticket in a year, we installed cruise control and ended the problem. It's a genuine convenience to set your speed and let the wonderful little electronic gadget hold it there for you. One speeding ticket will pay for it, too.

POWER WINDOWS. Pure decadent luxury? There are two valid reasons for power windows. The first may sound trivial, but for a long-leggedy beastie it's nice not to have that always-in-the-wrong-place window crank banging the knee.

The second reason is that power windows give the driver control of all of the windows in the car. No more having the kids roll down the back window when you have the air-conditioning on. Also, if the driver is short, reaching across to roll the opposite window down becomes possible. Power windows in domestic and Japanese cars are very dependable and give no more problems than do regular crank-ups.

POWER DOOR LOCKS. This is another luxury which is easy to get used to, particularly in a four-door, or even a full-size two-door which is difficult to reach across. The driver's door lock controls all the locks simultaneously, very handy when you are alone in the car. Again, a dependable option well worth having.

POWER SEATS. If you share your car with a driver of a different size, power seats are great. One of the best features of most power seats is the range of adjustment not possible with a manual seat. A deluxe power seat will go up, down, back and forth; the front and back of the seat can be raised independently of each other, yielding an infinite range of tilt angles; and the backrest angle is independently adjustable, too.

There are very few defective power-seat mechanisms. The only ones we've seen were on older GM cars which had not seen the best of care. Run all power seats through every range of travel while test-driving a prospective car. Make sure that the seats go up and down evenly, without one side going faster or farther than the other, resulting in a leaning seat.

Do not assume that because the driver's seat is powered that the passenger's seat is too. Lots of cars have a power seat on the driver's side only. The tilting backrest is an option independent from the power seat.

SPLIT-BENCH SEAT. Again, a wonderful convenience for drivers of disparate sizes. If one of you is six-four and the other five-two, a split bench seat makes it possible for the shorter of you to drive and still have the taller one in the front seat. Of course, individual or bucket seats will accomplish this as well, but the option of three across seating in front is lost.

POWER MIRRORS. Have you ever needed to adjust your right mirror as you were motoring down the highway? Power mirrors let you do so with ease. These are yet another used car bonus found

on a lot of high-end domestic and foreign cars. No
problems, either. They are even more dependable
than the manual remote-control mirrors whose long,
circuitous cables often fail.

REAR DEFROST. Great in almost any climate,
it ends forever not being able to see through a
fogged-up rear glass. Since a rear defrost system
consists of nothing more than an electrically-heated
piece of glass, it is totally dependable and maintenance-free.

You do need to be careful when cleaning the
window, however. Very thin wires are "printed" on
the inside of the glass and can be damaged with
scrapers or any other hard object. Best to use glass
cleaner and a soft cloth.

HIGH-DOLLAR STEREOS. If you happen to
get one for no extra charge on a used car, fine.
However, never pay extra for any kind of a radio on
a new car. Factory equipment car radios are usually
substandard, and always overpriced.

Bear in mind that for less than $500 you can buy
a really dynamite aftermarket, high-powered, full-
featured stereo system from any of hundreds of
discount sound-equipment stores. Many such stores
are able to install the equipment they sell, too.

This entire argument presumes that you want a
good sound system in your car. If you find the
sound of the no-extra-cost radio already in your car
satisfactory, leave it alone. But if you desire high-
quality sound equipment, don't expect to get it from
a factory radio. Some of the higher priced factory-
optional radios sound pretty good if you don't turn
them up too high, but even the better ones are
always more expensive than a superior after-

market system would be.

AIR-CONDITIONING. If we had to choose between a beat-up, 20 year-old clunker with air and a brand new, high-dollar cruiser without it, you can bet we'll take the clunker. With air, you have complete control of the climate in your car at all times.

Everybody knows the benefits of air-conditioning on hot days; passengers and driver alike arrive at destinations refreshed rather than sweaty and rumpled. But few people realize that air works well in cold and humid weather, too. Most people equate air-conditioning with "cold." Equating air-conditioning with "humidity-control" will make it a much more useful tool.

We live on the coast. Our humidity is usually quite high although the temperature rarely climbs above 70 degrees; we use the air all the time. Most automobile air conditioners allow control of the temperature of the "conditioned" air. Just turn on the air and set the temperature to warm. The temperature in the car might be the same as outside, but the humidity will be much lower.

Ever get into your car on a cold morning with a few other people and have all the windows fog up instantly? Just set the temperature at a comfortable level, turn on the air, and the windows will clear in seconds and stay that way.

There are myths afloat about air-conditioning requiring five or ten horsepower to operate, thus dropping gas mileage by several miles per gallon. Most air-conditioning compressor-pumps are driven by one small V-belt which can't possibly deliver any serious amount of power. A one or two mile-per-gallon penalty can be expected, depending on the car. Generally, the bigger the car, the less significant the drop will be. On a hot day, the mileage penalty for using the air will be about the same as that from the added wind resistance of having the windows open.

The only costs of having and operating an air conditioner are a negligible decrease in gas mileage, and the minor inconvenience to whom ever services your car—things are a bit more cramped in the engine compartment with the compressor in the way.

Air-conditioning compressors are very reliable and most can be expected to perform without a hitch to about 100,000 miles. It is essential to operate the air system frequently (at least a half-hour per month) to keep the seals from drying out and subsequently leaking.

If your car is a few years old and the air doesn't blow as cold as it used to, have the system serviced. The service should include checking the special compressor oil as well as recharging the refrigerant.

By now, it may seem that we advise getting every option available. Well, we do advise getting *just about* every option available. Options are one of the best reasons to buy a pre-owned car. Let somebody else pay for all the toys. In the used car market, most of the options cost very little extra. If you tend to replace your car every few years, you will find that a car without some options, especially air, can be difficult to sell, unless you are willing to let it go for less than market price. The newer the car, the worse the penalty.

On cars older than about five years, it's a buyer's market. Not even the infamous book shows a value increase for many options in the older cars. The older the car, the less extra you'll have to pay for the extras.

One more factor to figure in deciding what you need: is your best choice to keep the car you already have? There is an erroneous notion that 100,000 miles is a magic number that, when reached, suddenly determines that a car is worn out. But by now, you have probably recognized that service, maintenance, and the kind of driving done have more to do with a car's wear than just the number of miles.

Let's look at Elroy. He has a clean, dependable seven-year-old family car that he has serviced regularly. The car runs great, uses almost no oil, and has all the features he likes.

Then the odometer "rolls over" while he is cruising along in the middle of nowhere, and all the red lights on the dash come on at once. The stories about the magic number were true!

What happened? The belt that had driven the water pump and alternator since the car was new quit, and the original radiator hose blew. Why? As Elroy's odometer passed 90,000 miles he become less conscientious about servicing the car. He fixed only what needed fixing because he planned to get rid of it soon anyway. But he could have worked his own magic, and so can you.

Here's how. If you have a 100,000 mile car in generally good shape and you want another dependable 50,000 miles out of it, take it to your trusted mechanic with the following list, or do it yourself.

Unless you know that they are less than two years old, and/or have been regularly serviced according to manufacturer's recommendations, as necessary and if applicable:

- Replace all belts.
- Replace all radiator and heater hoses.
- Replace all four shock absorbers.
- Service all chassis lube points.
- Replace internal timing belts.
- Check & service cooling system.
- Check front end alignment.
- Change oil and filter.
- Tune engine.
- Service transmission.
- Adjust valves.
- Pack wheel bearings.
- Check and service brakes.
- Check tires' condition and replace as necessary.

Usually, the things that start going wrong with a car that make the owner nervous and are blamed on high miles, are simply caused by improper or infrequent maintenance. Hoses and belts are high on the failure list because they deteriorate in time and can fail even while they still look okay.

Replacing the worn out shocks on a high-mile car will not only extend the life of the tires and suspension components, it will also make the car ride again as it did when new.

The cost of service and maintenance of all the items on this list might run as high as $400-500, depending on the individual car. But that's pretty cheap for another 50,000 miles of trouble-free driving.

11. MILES PER GALLON VS. MILES PER DOLLAR

An economy car, by definition, should be economical, right? "Economical" implies that it will cost less than one which is less economical. Ask people what the term "economy car" means, and most will say, "Good gas mileage." But gas mileage alone is not the answer. If you are looking for an excuse to go out and spend a small fortune on a new mini-car, and you elect better gas mileage as the rationale, read on.

Let's use Joe and Mary Smith to illustrate the concept of an economy car. Joe and Mary now drive an eight-year-old Maxicruiser with a small V8 engine, automatic transmission, power steering, and air. It shows 87,000 miles on the odometer and is in better than average condition. It gets about 14 mpg in town and 20 on the highway.

Joe just got a new job (he's a computer programmer) and his Maxi was the only big, old car in the company parking lot. Joe needed a new car. In their quest for reasons to replace the Maxicruiser, Joe and Mary settled on better economy.

After several trips to various new and used car dealers, they finally decided on a three-year-old Minicar. The new ride was equipped with a five-speed transmission, a nice radio and air. It showed 30,000 miles on the odometer. Its price was $6,995, which they skillfully negotiated down to $5,995.

For their Maxicruiser, the dealer allowed them $1,000 against the purchase price of the Minicar. They were given the usual choice between an "extended warranty" or signing the AS-IS clause; they opted for the $400 warranty. After subtracting the value of their trade-in as their down payment, and paying outright for the license/tax/transfer fees, they signed a 36 month contract for a balance of about $5,400, drove their new car home, and proudly parked it in the driveway. They now had a car just like everyone else's in Joe's office parking lot.

Mary wasn't happy to find that their insurance premium had doubled because of the new car. Their agent explained that they had carried no collision on the old Maxicruiser; but since they were financing the new car, the lender insisted they carry collision. And as expensive as the newer cars were to repair (even a five mph tap on the front bumper of their Minicar could do over $1,300 damage), it just wasn't bright to drive without collision coverage, even if it were not required. Mary understood, but the extra $120 hurt just the same.

Since most of their driving was the commute to work and nearly all of it was on the highway, the Minicar was getting as much as 33 mpg. Maybe they could make their payments out of what they saved on gas, as the salesman had promised them.

Let's figure it out. The Smiths drove about 15,000 miles per year. The Maxicruiser averaged 17 mpg. 15,000 miles at 17 mpg comes to 882 gallons of fuel. At $1.50 a gallon, that's $1,323.

The Minicar uses 500 gallons annually at its average of 30 mpg. That comes to $750 for a year's supply of gas. So far, the Smiths show a savings of $573/year, or $48/month.

The added $120 for insurance coverage not needed for the old car drops their savings a bit: now they're down to $453/year, or $38/month.

Oh, yes, car payments. $5400 for 36 months, financed at a low 11%, comes to "easy monthly payments" of only $179.36.

But they are saving $38 a month, right? Right. So for driving a car half the size, half the comfort, and a fraction of the safety when compared to the sturdy old Maxicruiser, John and Mary pay only $141/month more to drive the Minicar. Keep track of this figure for a few moments—we'll get back to it.

Figuring only principle, interest and the down payment, they will have spent a total of $7,457 for the Minicar. After three years, they'll actually begin saving that $38 a month, because the Minicar will be paid off.

But will they be able to live with their basic Minicar for longer than three years? Won't there be sufficient social pressure by then to justify another new car?

Let's take a look at the two hypothetical cars after three years. Had they kept the Maxicruiser, it would now be showing 132,000 miles. If they had serviced the car properly during those miles, chances are good that they would have experienced no major problems. The Minicar would now be reading 75,000 miles. It, too, probably would not yet have needed any major repairs.

Let's figure in another expense: depreciation.

The Maxi was worth $1,000 three years ago. If it still looks and drives well, it's still worth $500. The Mini was worth $6,000 three years ago, or at least that's what John and Mary paid for it. At six years of age and 75,000 miles, it has a market value of about $2,000. The Maxi depreciated $500, the Mini, $4,000. It cost the Smiths $3,500 more in depreciation to drive the Minicar for three years than it would have to keep the Maxicruiser.

If you figure depreciation into the equation, John and Mary paid $238 every month for the privilege of driving the Minicar. All things considered, one has to question whether or not it was worth the extra expense.

Remember the original concept of making rational decisions. You must decide not only which car to buy, but whether to replace the old car in the first place.

If the Smiths could afford to shell out over $7,000 over the course of three years, if they had made the rational decision that they would rather spend the money on replacing their present car than on a down payment on a house or a lengthy vacation in the tropics, then there was nothing wrong with their purchase.

If, on the other hand, they purchased their Minicar the way most people do—blind to actual costs—they deprived themselves of things more important than having a car that blended better in the office parking lot.

One more "if": If John and Mary had opted for a new car, instead of one three-years-old, their expenses could have been thousands of dollars higher.

The lesson here is to figure in all the expenses, not just gas mileage.

The difference in gas mileage from one car to another is seldom a good reason to change cars. Certainly, if you are about to replace your present car anyway, and fuel economy is a factor, you would be wise to pay attention to the mileage figures of your prospective purchase. But buying a more expensive car simply because it gets better mileage requires some careful arithmetic to make an intelligent choice.

In today's used-car market, bigger cars, particularly older cars, are almost always bargains compared to the little fuel-efficient models. The bigger cars generally go farther before needing major repairs. If you have to pay a thousand dollars more for a miniature car than for a nice, big, comfortable cruiser in comparable condition, you might never save enough on gas to pay the difference.

Let's use another example. You need a car and you just happen to be in love with a mid-eighties full-size Olds. Your conscience tells you that you should buy a Honda to save money on gas. You drive 15,000 miles per year, mostly highway.

An '86 Olds with the overdrive transmission will get an easy 20 mpg. Let's give the Honda a break and say it will do 40 mpg. In 15,000 miles, the Olds would use 750 gallons of gas; the Honda 375. At $1.50/gallon, it would cost $562 more per year to drive the Olds. If you planned to keep either car for three years, you would have to buy the Olds for about $1,700 less than the Honda to come out even. Time to shop around.

Not everybody loves big cars; we do. If we had a specific amount of money available with which to buy a car, we would choose an older cruiser over a newer econo-car for the same amount of money.

Matter of fact, that is exactly what we do. Our family car has always been a loaded cruiser bought for peanuts because it showed at least 70,000 miles on the odometer. It was always selected because of its as-new condition and the obvious, and often documented, care that it received.

We have never had to do a major repair to any of these cars, and we have driven several of them, without a hitch, to well over 150,000 miles.

Whether your personal tastes dictate big cars, little cars or in-between cars, the same principles apply.

What counts is miles per dollar not miles per gallon.

Let's talk for a moment about ultimate miles per dollar. Did you know that there are lots of good, dependable cars available for less than $1,000? Even less than $500?

We have been joyfully driving cheap cars for years. Not because we can't afford to drive a car just like everyone else does, but because we enjoy squeezing all of those free miles out of a good piece of machinery.

Example: Back in 1984, we bought a beautiful 1971 Oldsmobile "98" sedan with every conceivable option (and they all worked) from another dealer for $450. This was not some kind of special dealer-to-dealer sale, either. Anyone off the street could have bought the car (whale, our neighbors called it) for the same price.

The Olds showed 97,000 miles when we bought it, was exceptionally clean, and ran like new. By 1988, we had logged another 60,000 miles on the car. During that time, we installed a new set of discount-store tires and a water pump. Our total expenses to date, including the price of the car, amounted to $750.

Unfortunately, about this time, we loaned the car to a friend who thoroughly trashed the still-beautiful-but-thin brocade upholstery on the front seat, and soon after that, the windshield developed a crack. It was time to move on. We sold it to a clunker dealer for $300.

Four years and 60,000 miles use of this ultra-comfortable cruiser had cost us $450. That's a lot less than most owners of new, itsy-bitsy, disposable mini-cars spend on their first year's interest. Miles per dollar.

Obviously, as auto dealers, we had available any number of shiny, late-model dreamboats to sport around in, and we did. But to stay in business, we had to turn a profit on these cars. What were we doing cruising around in a twelve-year-old car? Smiling.

If you apply the techniques in Chapters 14 and 15 in your search, you will be able to find any number of decent, presentable and dependable $500-$1,000 cars. One of the best things about a $500 car is that it cannot possibly depreciate more than $500, no matter what you do to it.

Matter of fact, any car which looks decent and runs well will likely always be worth $500. Your only expense of operation will be any required repairs. Again, if you apply your expertise in selecting such a car, there will be no repairs other than the nickel-and-dime stuff that occasionally happens to any car.

Not all cheap cars are huge-mobiles. There are lots of fifteen-year-old Toyotas, Mazdas, Datsuns, and the like, available in the under $1,000 price range, too. You do have to be more careful with the little ones, though. They are not as robust as the bigger cars, and when something does need to be fixed or replaced it will usually cost more. Old Toyota Coronas are a prime example of a durable Japanese car. It is not unusual for a reasonably cared-for Corona to go well over 100,000 miles before needing any repairs.

In our younger days, we drove nothing but older, excellent cars which we bought for next to nothing. Often we drove one for a few years and sold it for more than we had paid for it.

We regularly receive comments regarding our big old car, and how can we afford to buy gas for it. (Our current big old car is a thirteen-year-old Dodge.) It is a well-maintained, comfortable cruiser with all the toys, and it gets about 18 mpg. We paid $800 for it two years ago when it had 65,000 miles on it. We now live in a little coastal village and never leave here unless we absolutely have to, so we log less than 5,000 miles a year on the car.

The last person to berate us for driving a gas-guzzler had just shelled out a little over $7,000 for a new econo-mini-car which he claims gets 40 mpg. In the last two years, we have spent about $700 on gas for our cruiser. In the last two weeks the econo-car owner has spent three times that much on depreciation. When he reminds me that depreciation is non-polluting, unlike all that gas we burn, we wonder how much gas we would have to burn to equal the amount of pollution that was produced in the manufacture of his new disposable transportation appliance.

If your goal is the absolute highest attainable ratio of miles per dollar, as opposed to miles per gallon, there is no substitute for a good, old, depreciation proof, cheap car.

12. PLANNED OBSOLESCENCE

Planned obsolescence is not a new idea. Most people are aware of appliances that wear out on the expiration date of their warranties. But not all obsolescence deals with wear. Much of it is planned in style.

Remember in the early fifties when Chevrolet stunned the public with its brand new line of super-deluxe cars called Bel Air? Everybody had to have one. Then in 1958 they dropped the Bel Air's status by introducing the Impala. If you still had a Bel Air in your driveway in 1958, you obviously were on some kind of an embarrassing budget, because the Impala was the way to go.

And so it went. The Caprice. Then the Caprice Classic. And on it goes. Each few years, the top-of-the-line models get one-upped by another new name.

Yet, when prospective buyers go to look at the

new cars on the showroom floor or at gala annual auto shows, most of the cars are not new at all. They certainly are not the newest thing the industry could offer. The really new stuff, which is on the drawing boards right now, will not show up on the showroom floor for years. The whole game is a carefully thought-out scheme of long-term, planned obsolescence.

Allow us to offer examples of this standard, industry-wide practice. One popular Japanese automaker's favorite method is to introduce a brand-new, high-dollar sports model in, let's say, 1987 . . . .

It was a new number, so all the people who were obsessed with owning what's HOT! rushed to buy one. They hardly noticed that although these new cars looked really great, they were available in only three colors and with only a rather drab, grey interior. Didn't matter. Trendsetters told themselves, "I would really rather have it in blue with a black interior, but this is such a great looking car, and it's NEW. What the heck?"

But what happened in 1988? The same car, which was no longer new, appeared on the market in the dazzling array of colors that were available on every model of that maker's other cars in 1987. It was now available with all the interior color options, too.

As far as the manufacturer was concerned, they had introduced another "new" car. They did it by intentionally withholding colors from the first model which were available on the rest of their whole product line. Their experience had shown that a predictable number of people would buy the new car in basic grey, just because it was new. When that market dried up, they offered the full color line and opened their doors to a whole new arena of buyers.

The system works, and it works well. A lot of the people who bought the drab '87 model rationalized dropping another few thousand dollars in 1988 to buy the same car in the colors they would have liked, and which should have been available, in the first place.

And guess who loses if one of these new offerings turns out to be a lemon? The automobile industry has repeatedly been able to produce and sell products which fail prematurely and not be required to make good to their customers. And why should they? The customers just keep coming on back for more.

The public has never been much good at paying attention. It continually amazes us that people we know, folks who should know better, go out and buy cars which already have well-earned reputations for predictable, specific problems. All they would have to do is ask any good mechanic, "I'm thinking about buying a 1986 Ford Tempo. What can you tell me about their reliability?"

Or how about, "I like those Toyota sedans of the mid-eighties. Can you tell me any particular ones I should stay away from?" That's all it takes to save yourself the hassles and grief of buying a car that you can depend on to be a lemon, and offers another wonderful reason for buying a used car instead of a new one. Let someone else weed out the lemons for you.

Another example: One automaker built a

wonderful little four-wheel-drive vehicle, a humble little car when first presented in the middle seventies. In 1980 the company introduced their first really nice looking version of that car. The new line included a four-door sedan, a great looking two-door hardtop, a station wagon, and a hatchback. But of these, four-wheel drive was available only in the hatchback and wagon. The sedan and hardtop were front-wheel-drive only.

After a couple of years, a growing number of the marque's enthusiasts started saying it would be nice if the other models also came in a 4x4 version. But that didn't happen. All the folks who needed four-wheel drive and would have jumped at a hardtop or sedan had to settle for the wagon or hatchback.

Then in 1984, they did it! They made their public ecstatic with the introduction of 4x4 hardtops and 4x4 sedans. Again, a lot of buyers who had settled for their second choices in 1983, jumped in and bought yet another new car in 1984, purely in response to the manufacturer's carefully mapped out strategy.

What strategy?

1984 was the last year of the then-current body style. In 1985 the company introduced another completely "new" line of cars. For an automaker to sell the last year's run of an old body style while many are willing to wait for the new one, a gimmick is in order. They engineered the 1984 gimmick into their then-new line in 1980.

If you peek underneath even the very first hardtops and sedans that this automaker produced in 1980, you will see all of the attachment points and access holes for mounting the mechanical 4x4

116

components. These cars were designed from the outset for installation of four-wheel drive. The manufacturer merely waited until just the right time, the last year of production of that body design, to "introduce" a feature which was actually ready since the beginning.

This sales-boosting technique for a last-year model run is not unique to this automaker. Standard industry practice demands a powerful gimmick for the last year of a model run.

More often than not, this is accomplished with "special edition" models, most of which are identical to last year's cars but with added glitter. The glitter comes in many forms: fancy striping, special moldings, perhaps an interior unique to this model, a "special" or "limited edition" name tag, a package of formerly optional accessories newly included as standard, maybe even a turbocharger. But the end result is still the old car, the last of the model year run, once more disguised as something new.

Another scheme of planned obsolescence is the purposeful manufacture of a product so that it starts to look shoddy enough to encourage its owner to seek "new" again long before it begins to actually wear out or perform poorly.

For example, look at the "chrome" trim on and around the dashboards of most cars built within the last ten years. Examine all of the edges and ridges which look like chrome, or did when the car was new. Chances are, the chrome like substance is in good shape only where it never gets touched.

This "chrome" is a plating process which can leave such a thin film of metal on the surface that normal wiping with household cleaners will remove it. That's on the expensive models. On the cheaper ones, it's thin paint, which can also be wiped off—if it hasn't already worn off by the time you get it home.

If you can buy an inexpensive plastic kitchen gadget with a chrome finish that lasts for years without showing any wear, can it be accidental that the finish on exposed parts of your $18,000 car is so poor? The chrome was meant to glitter its way into your heart and wallet on the showroom floor; and to disappear right before your eyes soon after the purchase.

Don't believe us? Go to a pre-owned car lot and check out the "chrome" trim on a mid-eighties Cadillac Eldorado with a couple of years or 30,000 miles on it. Be sure you tell the salesman you're just looking. And look at what's left of the shine.

By the way, should you have a vehicle whose pretty glitter is still intact, be advised that cleaners such as 409 will remove a painted "chrome" finish quickly. If the chrome is real, it will take a little longer.

The best way to clean dashboards is with a very soft, clean cloth dipped in mild dishwashing detergent in a limited amount of warm water. It is really disappointing to be carefully cleaning the dash of your nearly new, not inexpensive luxury car and see yellow plastic appear where the chrome just was.

(Incidentally, when cleaning dashboards in general and instrument panels in particular, it is essential to use a damp, not wet cloth. Any excess moisture from the cloth is easily drawn up behind the plastic instrument covers and will leave a stain which can be removed only by removal of the cover, often a very time-consuming job requiring the use of special tools.)

And have you ever wondered whether it is simply

coincidence that gas prices and car sizes take frequent inversely-proportional roller coaster rides?

Remember the sixties and seventies, when cars kept getting bigger and bigger? The ads kept telling you that the new Whooshmobile was a whole foot-and-a-half longer than the opposition's newest monster; how impressed all your neighbors would be if you had one in your driveway. Cars got bigger until they became absurd. Vast expanses of gaudy colored sheet metal, some were not unlike circus floats. The roller coaster climbed up.

Gas prices started climbing, too. And climbing. And soon the car companies came to the rescue. Lucky consumers could suddenly trade in their whale-like cars on smaller ones and get better mileage. Only it wasn't that simple. The big old cars were safer, more comfortable, more powerful, and obviously more expensive. After having reached that plateau, drivers were reluctant to come down.

But obsolescence can be manufactured, too. Enter Madison Avenue. Advertising began to intimate that it was unfashionable to be seen in a big car. It soon became downright unacceptable. The used-car market was turned upside down, with prices dropping out the bottom on full-size cars. It was amazing to see a three-or four-year old Pinto sell for more money at the wholesale dealers' auction than a same year, full-sized, loaded Ford LTD! The roller coaster swooped down.

About the time the auto industry had saturated the market with socially acceptable teensy cars, gas prices started back down. And down. New ads declared that safety and comfort were certainly more important than trying to save a few pennies on gas. Mini-cars just weren't safe. Besides, the new, larger cars were getting better mileage than their previous generation.

Each model year saw the cars growing again. Each model year brought advertising which blatantly informed the car-buying public that the new car was more luxurious because it was nearly a foot longer than the one they claimed was the greatest thing on the road last year. The roller coaster was on its way back up.

The same thing happened with diesel cars. About the time that the gas prices really started soaring, Detroit introduced the diesel option. In theory, driving a diesel-powered car would save a pile of money. GM sold thousands of them before people started to realize that their ill-conceived, converted from gas engines were coming apart at the seams.

Not all diesel engines were poorly built, and at the height of diesel's popularity, most automakers were offering diesel engines in most of their product lines. Then through another amazing coincidence, just about the time that all the diesels that were going to sell were sold, the price of diesel fuel started going up until it cost as much or more than gasoline. Who in his right mind was going to hang onto a smelly, gutless, unreliable, noisy diesel, when he could drive a gas engine car for the same money?

In today's auto market, with few notable exceptions, a diesel engine is the kiss of death. At the auctions, when a diesel drives into the auction barn, almost everybody walks out. If a diesel car sells at all, it will usually bring half what the same unit would bring with a gas engine. And often, the buyer will be someone who will install a gas engine in the car and resell it at a comfortable profit.

How about the aerodynamic hype? Who knows when it actually started, but it does seem to work well. Not too many years ago, most cars were round. Some not unlike a worn bar of soap. Remember the Nashes of the fifties? Or the Ford Falcons of the early sixties? The reason? Aerodynamic efficiency.

Then the market needed a gimmick, and body lines started becoming more angular. Angular design went to almost absurd lengths, always proclaiming even better aerodynamic efficiency, and supporting claims with numbers that were less than meaningful to the general public.

About the time that the corners on our cars became sharp enough to pose a hazard, the aerodynamic efficiency boys must have figured out that they had been wrong all these years and what we really needed was the Ford Taurus. Now all of our cars are once again round, in the interests of attaining better . . . you guessed it, aerodynamic efficiency. Who is fooling whom?

The auto industry has the consumer well-trained to respond to its every suggestion. And the billions of dollars spent each year on advertising are paying big dividends. Car ads are no longer selling cars, they are selling lifestyles. When is the last time you saw any technical details offered in a TV ad for a car?

What you do see is beautiful people attracting more beautiful people with the cars they appear in. What would you do with all the money you'd save if you would change your philosophy from "Happiness is having what you want" to "Happiness is wanting what you have."

Advertising and planned obsolescence work together as a very effective team. America's merchandising system is based on these two premises, and not only in the auto market. The corporations start working on us when were babies. Have you looked at Saturday morning television lately and objectively observed how the advertisers are working on your children?

In spite of the fact that he has been well-counseled in the loopholes of truth-in-advertising, our teenage son is a ripe candidate for the system—a ready, willing and able supporter, a perfect consumer. He will spend hours looking at some new gadget in a catalog convincing himself that he really needs it. Then he'll save his hard earned money and eventually make the purchase.

For a while he'll love it to death, speak of it constantly. Until the new catalog shows up with the new model. Same exact gadget, but the chrome is in a different place. For reasons beyond us, it will be important to him to have the "new" one. The scene starts all over again.

"Different" is an important operative in the world of planned obsolescence. Most new cars are not new at all. Just different. A few trim items may have changed; just enough to let your friends know whether you still have last year's model.

Yesterday, I heard an ad on the radio which is typical of most advertising today: an emotion-filled 60 seconds of diatribe, with the end result of nothing at all having been said. A carefully-planned misrepresentation, an instrument to make you believe something other than what was actually said.

The scary thing is that I questioned several people who also heard the ad, and all "heard" what the ad implied, not what it actually reported.

Here is the ad: "City Chevrolet (not the real name) is having a sale like no other sale you've ever seen! Listen to this: City Chevrolet has a lineup of brand-new Chevy S-10 pickups that are selling for as much as $11,000 all over the country, and we are selling them for as little as $6,200!"

The folks I talked to actually "heard" this ad proclaim that City Chevrolet was offering to sell them the same vehicle which sold for 11 grand all over the country, for $6,200.

Just on the off-chance that you are not getting the picture, what was actually said in that ad was this: City Chevrolet will sell you a stripped-down version of the S-10 pickup for $6,200, its list price all over the country. Of course, they will also sell you a loaded version for $11,000, again, its list price all over the country. The key phrases here, as in most advertising, are "as much as" and "as little as."

Another commonly used gimmick-phrase, which makes the entire statement it's used in meaningless, is "up to . . . ."

For example, "Our entire inventory will be on sale this week only for discounts of up to 40%." What does this mean? Usually, it means that there will be one car, probably one so ugly that the dealer is sure nobody will buy it, discounted 40% from an inflated list price. The rest of the inventory will carry the "up to" discounts, like 10 or 20%. And even then, what does a discount mean if you don't know what the price was discounted from?

The high-powered, high-dollar advertising which so effectively hammers in the message that what we have isn't as good as what they offer is one of the many obstacles standing in the way of approaching a new-car purchase objectively. Don't be fooled. Buying a second-hand car in premium condition is a wise decision.

If you are still inclined to pay the enormous penalty necessary to own a new car just because you will then have something unique, be sure to read Chapter 13, "Special Interest Cars."

13. SPECIAL INTEREST CARS

O h, remember when you could buy a brand new Toyota Corolla or a Mercury Capri for $2,400? There were rumors that the auto industry was about to take the American public on the most outrageous roller coaster ride they had been on yet. Predictions from the ivory towers of Madison Avenue promised that cars would cost over $20,000 by 1990. These predictions were accompanied by statements that the whole scam would be so well pulled off that the public would fully accept those prices by then. Well, guess what?

You can get off the roller coaster. A special interest car is just one way to do it. And if you have ever had the inclination, there has never been a better time.

Regardless of how many thousands of dollars were spent on its optional extras, a new Toyota,

Oldsmobile or Audi is not distinctive or unique. It is hardly noticeable among the sea of others just like it when brand new, and nearly invisible a few months down the road. (Ever tried unsuccessfully to unlock your car in a supermarket parking lot only to discover that it wasn't your car, but just another clone?)

A new car is only new for a short period of time. Actually, as soon as you sign the papers and drive off, you are driving a used car. Want proof? Turn around and go back to the dealer. Tell him you just received notice that you are being transferred to Cairo and need to get rid of the car at once. You will be informed in no uncertain terms that you are now driving just another used car.

Contrary to popular myth, you can have your cake and eat it, too. If the ideas presented here make sense, but you feel that this objective and sensible approach to car buying takes out a lot of the fun, read on. If you find the system of planned obsolescence unacceptable, but an occasional car replacement seems unavoidable; if you are torn between the economic advantages and disadvantages of spending the money to do a major repair to your existing car, knowing that its market value will not support the expenditure; if you place a certain value on driving a car that doesn't look like everyone else's; if you would love to turn your transportation budget from a large liability into an attractive investment; and if you want to own an outstanding, eye-catching automobile that will never depreciate, then you are a candidate for a special interest car.

A special interest car can be both distinctive and

unique, and can become ever more so as it ages.

Special interest cars cover a wide range. In its most accurate definition, "special interest" means that the car is of special interest to collectors, which also implies that the car is somewhat rare and therefore pricey. In our discussion, we will broaden that definition somewhat to include also cars that might be of special interest to you alone. We do this not in an effort to irritate the collectors, but to simplify the language of our discussion.

The real special interest cars include such sought-after vehicles as the first Pontiac GTO's, the earliest Mustangs, "300 series" Chryslers, early Corvettes, '55 through '57 Chevy Nomads, and such esoterica. From there, the definition gets diluted somewhat to include just about any fifties Chevrolet and then to the top-of-the-line models of many older cars.

In our discussion, we will include any car which is of special interest to YOU. Your interest might be nothing more than nostalgia, or it might be based upon a long-standing admiration of a certain marque.

The advantages of owning a special interest car are several. First, in one fell swoop, you will have eliminated one of the most costly aspects of auto-mobile ownership: depreciation. One thing all special interest cars have in common is (assuming that they are maintained properly and not damaged) that they do not depreciate. On the contrary; they are investments. Of course, this presumes that you didn't pay too much for the car when you bought it; we'll go into this later.

Special interest cars are not necessarily old cars, either. For example, let's say that ever since Cadillac introduced its Seville in 1976, you have been lusting for one of these beautiful cars. The first Sevilles were a tasteful design devoid of the superfluous doodads GM started tacking on their cars in the seventies. They have become something of a collector's car, but to date have not appreciated much. This makes the car a "sleeper" as far as value is concerned. Extremely fine, well-maintained Sevilles can be found for under $5,000.

An automobile of this stature, particularly one in as-new condition, attracts more than its share of the exact kind of attention that most people expect when they bring home the brand-new car they just drove off the dealer's showroom floor. Today's new cars are so homogenous that a lot of folks feel it necessary to leave the price sticker in the window for months after the purchase just to make sure that all of their neighbors know that theirs is indeed a new car. Not necessary with a special interest car.

Another example: ever envied the guy who can afford to own a Jaguar or Mercedes? When you see a beautiful, shiny Jaguar sedan cruise by, do you know what year the car is? Couldn't that Jaguar, for all you know, be an exceptional example of a ten-year-old car? Many of the world's most prestigious cars are nearly ageless in their designs, meaning that a ten-year-old car looks enough like a two-year-old one that most people don't know the difference.

Many ten-year-old super-luxury cars, even those in exceptional condition with lots of useful miles left on them, can be purchased for less money than a new econo-can disposable car.

It's all a matter of personal taste. Some folks are embarrassed to be seen in anything but a "new" car, even if it is a bottom-of-the-line cheapo. Others would much prefer a classy, obviously well-maintained older car to any new car, not only because of the notoriety of being seen in and associated with such a vehicle, but also because owning and keeping up an older car is an effective way of sidestepping one of the most parasitic industries ever to become a part of our everyday lives.

With a well-chosen special interest car, there is never the question of whether or not it is financially prudent to make a necessary repair. Example: you own a six-year-old import in fairly nice shape. The car has 90,000 miles on it and the transmission is acting up. The repair shop informed you that it's just a matter of time before you will be facing a $500 repair bill. Decision time.

The car has already depreciated to under $2,000 (don't dwell on the fact that you paid over $8,000 for it), and that's assuming no transmission problems. Should you just sell it the way it is and take your lumps now, or bury yet another $500 in a dead horse?

If you opt to spend the money to fix the car, you will feel obliged to keep it for another few years to "get your money back." And what if another major repair rears its ugly head in the near future? It never ceases to be a dead-end street.

But if the car in question happened to be a 1965 Mustang, a 1979 Mercedes or Jaguar, a 1962 Chrysler 300, or any other excellent example of the car of your dreams, there is no question about repairs or the money spent on them. The funds spent on maintaining a special interest car are almost without exception, like putting money in the bank.

If this interests you, start reading the "collector's cars" section in the classifieds of any major newspaper. Or pick up a copy of *Hemmings Motor News*. (If you can't find it, write them at Box 100, Bennington, VT 05201.) Start looking over the prices of the cars and get a feel for what the values are. Of course, a classified ad will tell you little about the real condition of a car, but the overall picture will begin to become meaningful after researching it for a while.

It has been our experience that advertisers in *Hemmings Motor News* are generally more objective and less optimistic in describing their merchandise than are those who advertise in newspaper classifieds. Perhaps this is partly because *Hemmings* is read world-wide and mainly by auto enthusiasts.

Think about certain cars that you have admired for years. Wouldn't you finally like to own one? Look through the ads and see what they're going for.

The absolutely insane, ever increasing prices of new cars keeps making decent older ones worth more, so even a plain vanilla sedan that's ten years old but in pristine condition, is now worth an amazingly high proportion of what it cost new.

Special interest and/or collector's cars are becoming big business. A few years ago, only the true special interest cars appreciated rapidly. Now just about any interesting older car does. It is not too late to get in on the ground floor of this fulfilling adventure in auto ownership.

Unless you are already experienced in the restoration of old cars or have an unlimited budget, it is almost always better to buy a car which is either in excellent original condition or which someone else has had professionally refurbished, than to buy one needing complete restoration. The original cream puff is by far the best way to go, if you can locate one.

Nice originals are much easier to find in cars which have not yet made it to a highly sought after status. The chapter on checking out the mechanical and body condition of any used car applies to these cars as well, and it is not at all unusual to find that the owner of a special interest car has complete records of all service and repairs ever done.

If you desire to drive a prestigious automobile (cars are always referred to as "automobiles" when they are prestigious; if they are uncommonly prestigious, they are "motorcars"), you have two options. You can drop over $20,000 on a new cruiser that will soon be just another plain old used car, upstaged by all the new flash and worth half or less than you paid for it. Or you can go out and spend less on a beautiful, pampered, ten-year-old prestige ride like a top-of-the-line Mercedes, and put the rest in the bank to collect interest.

Your impeccable and impressive motorcar will continue to impress, and be a pleasure to own and operate for many years. The new $20,000+ car will decline in all areas: value, appearance and function. When it is only one model-year old, it will look just like hundreds of thousands of other used cars.

A look through an issue of *Hemmings* or the collector's cars classifieds will undoubtedly rekindle some pleasant memories. Even if you demand all the comforts and accessories offered in newer cars, remember that almost all of them were available in the expensive cars of ten, 20 and even 30 years ago.

Many 50's cars had air-conditioning and power-assisted steering, brakes, seats, and windows. Almost all high-end domestic cars of the sixties had all of these features available. And how long has it been since you've driven an older car? After getting used to smaller cars over the years, you might think you would not like a big car any more at all. But then again, you might.

"Sixties domestic" doesn't have to mean big, either. One particularly desirable sixties car is the Buick Skylark. Remember them? Looked a little like a reduced-size version of a full-size Buick, except that the designers did such a fine job that the car didn't have that shrunken, miniature look that many similar efforts have produced.

Skylarks were available in '61 through '63, in sedans, convertibles, hardtop coupes and wagons. The '61 and '62 are the most sought-after, but are still available in primo condition for less than $5,000. Compared to what they cost new, that may seem a bit much. But compared to what you can buy in a late-model ordinary-just-like-everyone-else's car for the same money, it's a bargain. An ordinary $5,000 used car will be worth $500 in a few years, but the '62 Skylark will just keep appreciating.

If your desires run to something a little more exotic, like an XKE Jaguar or even a Triumph TR6 or MGB, make sure that you have the car gone over with a fine-tooth comb. Make absolutely certain that you are not looking at a badly rebuilt wreck. Remember, you are buying this car as an investment. These cars, particularly the Jaguar, can be expensive to maintain. But even so, purchased for a fair price, they are still an excellent investment.

Many marques of older cars enjoy such popularity that owners form organizations to promote keeping them on the road forever. Membership in these clubs is highly recommended, for they supply fine parts and information resources as well as camaraderie and support.

Chapters 14 and 15 will guide you through the process of checking out a prospective purchase. The techniques are the same as for a newer car. However, since the likelihood of reconditioning becomes greater as a car ages, we strongly recommend that you seek the counsel of professionals in making a final evaluation, particularly if this is an expensive purchase and/or one which you aspire to keep for years.

An obvious question asked by those just becoming interested in special interest car ownership is, "What happens if I ever need something major, like an engine, for an out of production car?"

OK, say you own this absolutely wonderful 1954 Studebaker Commander Starlight Coupe, and it needs an engine. Now what? Not many dismantlers are likely to have in stock a fresh, low-mileage Studebaker engine. You have at least two alternatives. One is, of course, an overhauled engine. The other is a nice, fresh, low-mileage engine from an entirely different make of car.

The very thought of an engine swap on any collector car is enough to make many enthusiasts violently ill, if not violent . . . but please read on.

Adapters are available which can bolt together some of the most unlikely combinations of engines and transmissions. Your local auto parts store probably has a catalog of these and can order one for you. There are whole adaptor kits available for some of these swaps. They include the engine to transmission adaptor, the engine mounts, and any other hardware needed to make the swap. Admittedly, engine swapping is something which must be done by a competent mechanic. We suggest that you never engage the services of a mechanic who has not successfully done other swaps or who expresses disdain when approached with the possibility. Clearly, this kind of work is best done by someone who enjoys doing it.

If you are mechanically competent, have the facilities to do the job, and enjoy working on your own car, you could probably do the job yourself. It is time consuming simply because of the little nit-picking details like adapting and re-routing fuel lines, throttle linkage and such. The end result, however, can be very rewarding and worth all the soon-forgotten frustrations and damaged knuckles.

An important side benefit of doing your own work, be it an engine swap or just maintenance, is that you become more familiar with your automobile. This familiarity produces in most people a feeling for the car which lets them know immediately if something is not right, and a competence in determining what it is.

Another, and often preferred, solution to engine swapping is to use an engine/transmission package and forget about adapters. This way, you will need to adapt transmission mounts as well as engine mounts, but you will have dispensed with any intangibles of mating an engine to a non-matching transmission.

We have seen quite a few of these installations

where the only change necessary to mount the new transmission was to drill new holes in the transmission mounting crossmember.

It's wise to remember that engine swapping in some special interest cars can seriously reduce their value. If yours is simply an older car whose main value is derived from its excellent condition and your enjoyment of ownership, this would not apply. But installing the "wrong" engine in a genuine collector car would be a wise choice only if you planned to keep the car forever, didn't care about the car's dollar value, and/or if you were immune to the disparaging remarks from every collector car buff you will ever encounter.

We endured such disparagement for years while driving a remarkable Jaguar Mark X with a Chevrolet engine and transmission. Installing the Chevy components dramatically improved the performance, gas mileage, and handling of the Jaguar. It also turned it into a very dependable machine, something Jaguars, particularly older ones, are rarely accused of being.

Hemmings Motor News is also an excellent resource for parts—anything from frames to door handles. The publication lists each marque in its own section, and divides that section into subsections for parts and cars. Chapter 17 of this book covers dealing with auto dismantlers and their hotline access to parts all over the country.

Assuming that a swap is out of the question, let's discuss the other alternative, that "O" word, the overhauled engine. (See Chapter 17 again for an indepth discussion on overhauls.) Since we have not yet seen an acceptable overhauled engine, we are not in a position to offer any referrals. But in an effort to be of some assistance, we interviewed some collector car people. They all were of the same opinion—it is extremely difficult to find a shop capable of doing satisfactory overhauls. Most of them did, however, have a favorite; a shop which was the only place they would go for an overhaul.

Our suggestion is to use this same resource when you decide you need an engine rebuilt. Find a collector and ask for a referral. How do you find a serious collector? Many auto parts stores can direct you to customers who are old car enthusiasts. You can always talk to the owner of a nice, older car you happen across in a parking lot. Most of these folks are happy to help out another car buff. And special interest or vintage auto shows are two of the best places to get lots of feedback.

But make sure that you get engine-overhaul referrals from collector car enthusiasts, not hot-rod or racing people. There are distinct differences between the disciplines involved in building engines whose chief focus is maximum power and those who seek quiet dependability. Always go to the guy who is the specialist in the field that interests you.

When you find your prospective overhaul shop, talk to the owner/manager and ask to see the machine shop. You can usually tell a lot about the care which goes into a person's product by observing the condition of his work space. Ask for a cursory tour of his machine shop and an explanation of the processes your engine will go through in its overhaul. Before signing the work order, get in writing a list of the new parts which will go into your overhaul regardless of the condition of the existing parts.

In summary, ownership of a special interest car can be an extremely rewarding experience in many regards. Owners of these cars are generally immune to the rantings of the auto-advertising world. They are immune to planned obsolescence. They get to sidestep one of the costliest factors of car ownership—depreciation.

They don't have to tolerate the high-tech nonsense of all new cars, all the computer gadgetry which makes it impossible to maintain their cars themselves. They don't have to endure the cheap, flimsy construction, shoddy assembly, and ultra-complex, computer-controlled operational systems evident in so many new cars. They have the most noteworthy ride on the block this year, next year, and on down the line.

14. CHECK IT OUT—BODY

Are you ready for a horror story? Our own sister and her husband (not inclined to listen to advice) bought an eight-year-old Ford wagon, loaded with options. They paid over $4,000 for a very tired, 140,000 mile turkey after the dealer convinced them that the miles were correct at the 40,000 showing on the odometer.

It took us only a five-minute cursory examination to determine that the miles were over (the odometer had passed 100,000 and had started over). All the indicators were there. The upholstery and carpets showed more wear than they would have in 40,000 miles of use, the cap covering the brake pedal was worn through to the metal in places, and every cosmetic detail of the car showed lots of wear.

Even if the car really had gone only the indicated miles, the obvious wear and tear would have ruled it out as a likely candidate for purchase.

Then we looked under the hood. The transmission fluid smelled distinctly burned. Ford C6 transmissions do not show burned fluid (bad clutches) at 40,000 miles; however, they often do at 140,000 miles. The air-conditioning compressor was making some pretty awful noises. Again, a clear symptom of lots of miles. These compressors often need an overhaul, or at least bearings, at 80,000+ miles, but never at 40,000.

The engine also sounded very tired. Big V8 engines with low mileage and in good shape are very quiet. This one made lots of mechanical noise. Pulling the PCV (positive crankcase ventilation) valve out of the valve cover revealed way too much smoke (any is too much for a 40,000 mile car).

It had also suffered obviously from a major collision at some point in its history. And although evidence of improperly repaired major collision damage was no reflection on the mileage of a car, it was certainly a clear reason to reject it.

The first trip taken in this car cost its proud new owners about $1,000 in repairs. The air-conditioning compressor seized, the catalytic converter plugged up, and there were other minor problems as well. Then, the alternator went out.

A few months later, someone sold them yet another $120 alternator, claiming that whoever had sold them the last one had installed the wrong unit. They spent hundreds on the cooling system, which still overheats.

On another trip, they shelled out an amazing $900 to get the transmission overhauled. They are, as the saying goes, buried in the car, and they put another

$3,000 into it when the inevitable engine failure occurred, stranding them 1,000 miles from home.

It would have been so easy to avoid the whole experience if they had paid attention before they bought the car. That is what this book is all about: selecting a car that doesn't need a mechanical failure insurance policy.

You've spent a lot of time doing constructive, objective reasoning. You have kept in mind the role your emotions will play in the selection of your new or used car, and you feel comfortable knowing that your decision will be based on good judgment.

The body, paint, and general appearance of the car present its first impression. Now is the time to learn some important techniques to help you find the car you really want—a car that has received proper maintenance and is exactly what it appears to be. You don't want to end up with a lemon disguised carefully, possibly even professionally, to look like a peach.

Let's start with the question you'll likely ask first, "Has it ever been wrecked?"

Most buyers have been programmed to reject a car automatically if they find out it has been wrecked. But at the same time, who would dream of discarding a two-week-old new car just because it had been involved in a fender bender?

It's all right to wreck one's own car and have it repaired just like new. So why is it unacceptable to buy a car that someone else crunched? It isn't. Just because a car has been wrecked does not necessarily mean that the car wasn't repaired. You can use the techniques that follow to check repairs done on your own car, too.

Wrecks happen in many degrees. Some can be repaired properly by the average body shop, and some shouldn't be repaired at all. The first and most obvious clue to body repairs is found in the paint which covers those repairs. If a car has been completely refinished, it is usually easy to tell. With few exceptions, most body shops are pretty sloppy at masking (taping off those areas that are not supposed to get painted, such as glass, moldings, and other trim). This lack of craftsmanship presents the most obvious indication of a repaint. Lack of craftsmanship in the paint may well indicate lack of craftsmanship in the repair.

When a car is painted at the factory, the body is devoid of all trim, moldings, glass, nameplates, bumpers, etc. Therefore, if you spot any body color paint on any of these items, anywhere on the car, you know it's repaint.

On a complete repaint, this evidence is likely to be all over the car. Any areas which are difficult or time consuming to mask, will generally have paint on them—at least along the edges closest to the body. Of course, the better the paint job, the neater the masking is likely to be.

Even on the uncommonly well-masked car, lifting up the edges of any soft trim (rubber seals around glass and some moldings) will usually reveal the evidence you're looking for. Slide a fingernail under the edges of soft trim here and there, and look for the tell-tale edge of new paint.

Another product of sloppy masking is overspray. Overspray is any paint which reached any place it wasn't supposed to go. Open the doors and inspect along their inner edges. Look for body color paint on the black rubber door-seal gasket. Look especially at the door jamb. It should show only clean, shiny, factory paint. If there is fuzzy, dull paint showing around the edges of the jambs, there has been some repainting done.

Open the trunk and look for the same thing. The black rubber gasket which seals the trunk lid to the body will have no body color overspray on it unless it is carelessly masked repaint.

Again, when a car is painted at the factory, there are no locks, latches or strikers installed, so overspray on any of these parts also indicates repainting. There are exceptions to this (notably on GM cars, many of which are painted with these lock parts in place, rendering the lock parts completely painted with body color).

Now look under the hood—a classic area of sloppy or non-masking. Most cars have rubber bumpers or pads along the inner edges of the fenders. These pads are rattle and vibration dampers, and contact the hood when it is closed. There should be no paint on these parts, nor on any other rubber pieces or gaskets around the hood opening. Some shops are so careless about engine compartment protection that the entire engine and everything else under the hood will be covered with a fine dusting of body color.

If the car has a cowl screen (a panel, usually with slots or a grille of some sort, between the back edge of the hood and the bottom of the windshield), look into the openings. Cowl screens are time consuming to mask or remove and will often show evidence of repainting. If there is a screen or mesh panel visible through the openings in the cowl screen, it should have no body color paint on it. Neither should the windshield wiper mechanisms visible through it.

"Spot painting" is the refinishing of a small area—just enough to cover the repair or replacement of a panel, such as a fender or door. Spot painting is a little harder to detect, because there isn't as much of it. Unless a spot job is very well done, it can be most easily found by squatting down at the front or back of the car and looking carefully down the entire side, one panel at a time. Look for any irregularity: something in one area which is not the same as the rest of the surface.

Just about any unrepaired car will have body panels which are smooth, shiny, and uniform. If there has been a less-than-perfect repair made, that area will show small ripples in the body surface, and/or a different texture in the paint.

For example, if you catch a reflection in a piece of glass or a mirror, it is perfectly smooth. The reflection of an object with straight lines will have straight lines as well. Few cars have finishes this smooth, but many come close.

The trick to finding body or paint repairs is to catch reflections. Reflections should be similar everywhere on the car. If one particular area gives a dull or fuzzy reflection, or if straight lines reflect wiggly, they reflect a repair.

Another common tell-tale of bodywork is "sandscratch"—fine sanding marks in or under the paint, showing that preparation of the undercoats wasn't done properly. The sanding then shows through the finish.

Again, just because a car has had a minor fender-bender, it is not necessarily a candidate for rejection. What you are looking for is evidence of bodywork which will serve as clues to finding major repairs. Often, finding a simple thing like overspray or sloppy masking will prompt a more thorough investigation which reveals serious hatchet-work where somebody thought nobody would look.

The more serious collision repairs, if poorly done, will usually reveal themselves in ill-fitting doors, hoods, and deck (trunk) lids. Generally, you may assume that wherever you see a wider space between any two panels at one end than the other, something underneath is bent.

For example, if the gap between the front door and the fender is an eighth of an inch wider at the top than it is at the bottom, something is wrong. They don't put them together that way at the factory—with very few exceptions, that is. (Late sixties and early seventies GM and some Chrysler cars of that era were notorious for ill-fitting panels.)

You will almost never find any foreign car with less than perfect panel alignment. Even bottom-of-the-line Japanese cars are impeccable in fit and finish.

The gaps between each two panels should be the same width throughout the gap, and consistent from one panel to the next. If you find a vehicle with a space wider at one end than at the other between the hood and the fender, or the fender and the door, or the door and the rear quarter panel, or anywhere else, there is some structural damage hiding underneath. The only reason for such a misalignment in external sheet metal panels is a misalignment of the structure which supports them.

Another place to look for panel misalignment is

in their surfaces relative to each other. For example, on a four-door sedan, if the doors are flush at the top but the front door sticks out a quarter of an inch farther than the rear door at the bottom, something is seriously wrong. If this kind of misalignment appears in several places on the car, it is likely a "repaired" rollover in which the entire body structure is still twisted.

The door-to-fender, door-to-door, and door-to-quarter panel alignment should be nearly perfect on just about any car which hasn't been wrecked. No panel will stick out from its neighboring panel at the top or bottom on a car which has not been crunched.

To speak of perfect alignments between body panels may seem nit-picky, but it is often this clue which reveals "rebuilt totals" that should never have been rebuilt, or at least should have been rebuilt by someone competent to do the job. A qualified craftsman with the right tools and adequate expertise can do amazing repairs on a bent and twisted car. Many seemingly unrepairable wrecks can be repaired to as-new specifications.

The operative phrase here is "can be." Many minor wrecks are "repaired" to disguise the damage. The car may look satisfactory to the uneducated eye, but it can also be structurally unsound and unsafe.

On most newer cars, it doesn't take much of a collision to bend a frame. As a matter of fact, most newer cars don't have real frames at all. What serves as a frame is merely an assembly of various small "reinforcement panels" welded together to be strong as a unit.

Many of these individual pieces are not much heavier than body sheet-metal and depend completely upon proper assembly techniques to perform as designed. Any improper repair welds, can severely impair the integrity of the entire structure. Only well-trained craftsmen using the proper equipment can satisfactorily repair most late-model unit-body cars.

Consider this: a car survives a front-end collision, but the front of the frame gets bent upward on the driver's side. The body shop tries to straighten the frame, but lacking either the measuring tools, the expertise to use them, or the desire to do it right, the frame man doesn't get the frame rail pulled down quite far enough before he turns the car over to the body man.

The body man hangs on a new fender. When he installs all the bolts which hold the fender on, he notices that even though the fender lines up at the top, the space between the fender and the door is too wide at the bottom. (This is because the inner fender structure which supports the fender is up too high in front. The frame is still too high in the front.)

The body man goes back to the frame man who says, "It's good enough, just make it work." So the body man tries to even-out the error by making the space a little too tight at the top and a little too big at the bottom. The painter finishes the job, the wheel alignment technician fudges to compensate, the customer accepts it because he doesn't know any better, and another crooked car gets back on the road.

In most cases there is no way to align the front end of a car properly if the frame is bent. Most people don't notice the difference and will blame their tire shop for the excessive or unusual wear on their tires.

Some kinds of bad bodywork don't matter much—they only look bad to the trained eye, but other bad bodywork can seriously compromise the safety of the vehicle. All bad bodywork depreciates the value of a car.

We've seen bent frame cars where the error was so extreme that the bodyman loosened both doors on the damaged side, and adjusted them to average out the error down the whole side of the car. All of the spaces between each two panels were a little wider at the top than at the bottom, but there was no glaring error in one place.

We've also seen a few "repairs" where the repairman ended up with a panel misalignment he couldn't get rid of, and actually shifted the error back to an undamaged part of the car! For example, if a car is hit in the front, and the repairman can't get the gap between the front fender and the front door quite even, he simply loosens both of the doors on that side and shuffles their adjustments to make the error appear between the rear door and the quarter panel. Chances are excellent that the customer won't even look back there; the car was hit in the front. Believe it or not, this is common practice in many body shops.

Exactly what constitutes bad bodywork? When your car is involved in an accident, you take it to a body shop to be repaired. In theory, the goal of repair is to make the car look like it did before it was hurt. In other words, when the job is done, there should be no evidence of a repair having been made. If the repair is visible, it is unsatisfactory.

Of course the exception is a repair made to a vehicle with oxidized or faded paint, or one which

147

has already been blessed with an edgy repaint. But when dealing with a car which has the original finish in well-maintained condition, a visible repair is in fact, bad bodywork.

It is possible to repair even a badly damaged car properly. Evidence of quality repair work can be seen in the shops of the rebuilders of valuable antique and special interest cars. These cars are worth repairing, and their owners know that the value of the car will be seriously depreciated if the repair is not done properly.

Aircraft repairs present another example. Damaged airplanes don't get thrown on the scrap heap. They are simply too valuable. They get disassembled as far as is necessary to repair them to as-new condition.

The trick in getting an automobile repaired properly is to find someone with the talent, equipment, and desire to do the job right, and to be willing to spend the money for a proper repair after juggling all the figures with the insurance company. (Did you read Chapter 7?)

For a number of reasons, checking out a car in the rain is a bad idea. Even an expert cannot determine the condition of the finish, body and paint work, of a wet car. Neither can you detect a sand-pitted windshield in the rain. And standing in the rain puts unwarranted pressure on you to skip elements of your inspection. The extra noises involved in driving a car in the rain, road noise, wipers, and the rain itself, camouflage sounds you might hear on a clear day.

Be sure to examine the windshield in good light. Look for chips and little cracks coming from the corners. Especially at a dealer's lot, if there are any stickers on the windshield, look behind them for cracks, no accusation aimed at anyone intentionally placing a sticker over a windshield flaw.

Small cracks never get smaller—they invariably grow. Windshield replacements are very spendy, at the least several hundred dollars.

Examine the interior, as well. There is no excuse for a shoddy interior in what is being advertised as a well-maintained car. We have seen many, many cars with well over 100,000 miles on them with interiors so fresh that they could hardly be told from new.

Sit in the driver's seat and pay attention to comfort. You may be married to this car for a while, so make sure it feels good from the driver's seat. Does the seat seem to sag too much under your weight? Does the driver's side sag more than the right seat? If so, the car either had an inordinately heavy owner or it has logged lots of miles.

Check the overall condition of the upholstery. Look at the armrests and any other areas that get most of the wear. Check also the armrests in the back seat. It is common practice to switch armrests front to back when they are interchangeable, because it freshens up the ones most people look at and who ever examines the back seat?

If there are mats on the floor, look underneath each. Most sellers will not cover carpet in great shape with a set of floor mats.

How does the brake pedal look? The gas pedal? Clutch, if there is one? Does the wear correspond with what you would expect for the mileage shown? If a 50,000 mile car has a new pad on the brake pedal, find out why.

Open and close the doors, both gently and firmly. Do they close tightly? They should close easily and be firmly latched when shut. A driver's door which drops from its latch when opened, or which has to jump up even slightly when being shut is a sign of lots of use. Either the car has lots of miles on it, or the door was used a lot, as in much short-run city driving—the hardest kind of use.

Don't forget to look up, too. Is the headliner intact? Discolored with tobacco smoke? Check the package shelf and rear roof—pillar areas which often get serious sun rot even when the rest of the interior is still in good shape.

Try all the seat belts or whatever kind of restraint system the car offers. These items are spendy to replace, and most cannot be repaired.

Try the radio. Turn it up and try all of the speakers, but don't leave it on while you are test-driving the car. Some car sellers, individuals or professionals, will intentionally leave the radio on to divert your attention or to drown out funny noises.

Check the condition of the power accessories. Try all of the windows and all power seat functions. Make certain that the air-conditioning blows ice cold air when it is turned to its coldest setting. Forget that you might never want it that cold. If it doesn't blow ice cold at its coldest setting, you're looking at a repair bill in the future.

Remote mirrors? Make sure that they work, too. It may sound petty to check all of these small details, but it won't seem so later when you have to foot the bill for repairs. You might as well let the seller know that you know what he's trying to sell you. It can't hurt your bargaining position.

15. CHECK IT OUT—MECHANICAL

Now that you know what you're looking for, and out for, the first thing to remember, is that you should ignore everything that the salesman has to say. He is not legally liable for anything he tells you, so to listen to him is to divert your attention from the issue at hand: inspecting the car.

Use your own judgment or that of the expert you brought with you. (And by expert, we mean just that: someone thoroughly familiar with the workings of an automobile. It is important that you not rely on assumed expertise.)

You can assume that everything the salesman tells you is a lie, a diversion, or both. This is unfair to the salesmen with integrity, but their numbers are small enough to validate all doubt. Even the Federal Government has acknowledged that it is standard procedure for auto salesmen to lie as part of their pitch. (See Chapter 5.)

So where do you begin? How about a walk around inspection. You've already looked over the body, but now pay particular attention to the tires. Ideally, the tires should all be worn evenly and should reflect the mileage shown on the odometer. For example, if you are looking at a 20,000 mile car which is sporting brand-new tires, something is probably wrong. No car that you want to be the next owner of wears out a set of tires in 20,000 miles.

Most cars in normal use will, assuming that the tires have been rotated as per manufacturer's recommendations, get at least 35,000 miles out of a set of tires. Some get 50,000. Use these figures as a guide to determine whether or not the tires match the miles.

If the tires show any abnormal wear on one side or the other, especially the outside, suspect either very hard driving or an out-of-alignment front suspension. Don't just look at the front tires, either. It is common practice to put the best two on the front and the edgy ones back where they will be less likely to be examined.

Make absolutely certain that there is no mix of bias-ply and radial tires on the car. Mixing bias-ply and radial tires causes a very unsafe condition. It's not something you will be likely to find, but it does happen.

If everything looks good so far, check the engine. Many dealers, and some individuals, will start their cars each morning to warm them up so that they will crank over easily for customers. If you buy a previously warmed-up car, you might have a big surprise in store for you the first time you try to start it cold.

Make sure you are starting a cold engine. Before getting in to start it, open the hood and put your hand on the radiator. It should be cold. If it is not, be aware of the possibility that the car had been warmed up earlier to disguise cold starting problems.

In many newer cars the radiator is nearly inaccessible, so check for engine heat on any portion of the engine block or cylinder head.

When you get in the car, turn on the ignition, and, again, before starting the engine, observe the gauges or warning lights. If there are no gauges for oil pressure, engine temperature or charging performance, there will be warning lights which are sometimes referred to as "idiot lights." They should come on when the ignition is first switched on.

If any of the warning lights fail to light when the ignition is turned on, there is a problem. It could be any of several things: a burned-out bulb (not likely), a problem in the component that the light is a warning for, or the light could have been disconnected in an attempt to hide such a problem.

Since almost nobody checks these lights before starting the engine, it is easy to disable the oil-pressure light, for example, to disguise the fact that the oil pressure is so low that the light won't go off when the engine is started. (If we sound particularly distrusting, let us assure you that all of the tricks outlined in this book are in common use in the car business. And not just by little, low-budget dealers, either.)

Start the engine. Now go back to those warning lights. If everything is operating normally, the warning lights will go out as soon as the engine comes to life. The oil-pressure light should go out as soon as the engine is cranked over. If the oil-pressure light comes on occasionally at idle after getting the engine thoroughly warmed up, you have an indication of a tired engine.

This light should never come on, not even flicker, while the engine is running. The only exception is in a thoroughly warmed-up engine at idle with the air-conditioning turned on, causing the engine idle speed to be very low. There is still an indication of a problem here, but it could be in the device which speeds up the idle when the air-conditioning compressor comes on rather than excessively low oil pressure. If you do experience an occasional flickering of the oil light under these circumstances, turn off the air. If the resulting increase in engine speed doesn't turn off the light, go look at another car.

If the car has a real oil-pressure gauge instead of an idiot light, the oil-pressure gauge will immediately read at the high end of its scale when the engine comes to life (assuming that the engine is cold).

The ammeter will go to full charge and then in a few moments start to come back closer to the middle. A voltmeter will go up to the top end of its scale, somewhere around fourteen or fifteen volts depending of the individual gauge and the car.

The charge-indicator light might come on occasionally at idle, especially with a heavy load on the electrical system. For example, with headlights, wipers, and the heater all going, it would be fairly normal on some cars for the charge light to come on at a low idle. It should go off as soon as the engine speed is increased.

The temperature gauge shouldn't do much of anything at all. The engine-temperature warning light comes on only when the temperature has risen to a dangerous level, well above the normal range of operation.

Gauges have it all over warning lights. Gauges will warn you of impending problems; the lights generally don't come on until the problems are extreme.

Immediately shut down the engine to avoid serious damage if either the oil-pressure or the temperature lights come on while driving.

Once when driving a nearly-new Buick Riviera at freeway speed, the "hot" light came on. Before we could stop the car, the engine had seized. Had this car been equipped with gauges, we would have been warned of the problem in advance by seeing the temperature start to climb above its normal operating range. The ideal setup would be a light which alerted you to an impending problem, and a gauge with which you could monitor the situation.

Most drivers hardly ever look at their gauges. It is easy to take the amazing dependability of the average car for granted. If your car has gauges instead of idiot lights, try to make a habit of periodically glancing at the instruments. When this becomes a habit, it takes only a scan of the panel to see if everything is normal. You don't need to "read" each gauge.

For example, when you become familiar with your particular car, you might know to expect the temperature gauge to be just to the left of vertical, the oil pressure gauge to point straight up, the ammeter or volt meter to point slightly to the right of center, and so on. When this instrument scan becomes habit, any gauge which is registering even a slightly different from normal reading will catch your attention.

Habitual scanning has saved the day for us several times. Once in the middle of the night in the middle of nowhere, we were driving a car we had grown accustomed to, and in one of our every-fifteen-minutes-or-so scans, we picked up on an irregular reading of the temperature gauge. We knew the normal reading of this gauge was straight up (180 degrees, in this instance) and that it never deviated from that reading in any kind of normal weather and driving.

When we saw the gauge showing 190 degrees, we knew something was wrong. We watched it carefully for another few minutes and as soon as we confirmed that it was indeed climbing, we pulled over to the side of the deserted road. A check of the engine (with the flashlight we always carry) quickly showed the problem: a water-pump bolt was loose and leaking coolant.

Normally, a coolant leak is easily detected by the smell. This one was low enough on the engine that it went straight down and didn't drip on anything hot. There was no warning except for the reading on the temperature gauge.

With the bolt tightened (we also always carry a few basic tools in the trunk), we were able to drive on, carefully, to a tavern at which we were able to get water.

The point here is that if we had not been monitoring the gauges periodically, we would not have known about the leak until it was too late to do anything about it. And an idiot light generally won't come on until the temperature is so high that the engine must be shut down NOW in order to prevent serious damage.

If the car you're examining has gauges, check them both before and after starting the engine. Make sure that the oil-pressure and engine-temperature gauges read zero or are at the bottom of their ranges of operation. If there is an ammeter, it would read zero in the middle, "plus" or "charge" on the right side of the scale, and "minus" or "discharge" on the left. It should be centered on zero with the engine off. If there is a volt meter (more common on newer cars), it should read zero.

Why check the gauges with the engine off? More deceit, that's why. Again, most people never look at the gauges before starting the engine, making possible little tricks like this: We once bought a really nice Subaru wagon at a dealer auction. Of course we checked the oil-pressure gauge while driving the car on the test track. It looked great. We got the car home before noticing that the oil pressure read 50 pounds pressure whether the engine was running or not. Someone had taken the cover off the instrument panel and stuffed a carefully-trimmed wedge from a paper match under the needle on the gauge so that it stayed at 50 pounds. He assumed, correctly, that a buyer would not bother to observe the oil-pressure gauge unless the engine was running.

As it turned out, the Subaru needed only a new oil pressure sending unit. The engine was fine. But someone had gone to the trouble to do the dirty deed.

Another trick which works on many cars is to run the engine at a high enough speed to get whatever reading is needed on the gauge, and then pull the instrument circuit fuse while holding the reading. Instant permanent oil pressure! But detectable if you look at the gauges before you start the engine.

As the engine warms up, the oil pressure will drop slightly, the temperature gauge will start to climb to the middle of its "normal" range, and a voltmeter reading will taper off somewhat. A hard drive will allow the gauges to tell volumes about the condition of the engine.

A hot engine should still show normal-range oil pressure. An oil-pressure reading of less than 20 pounds at idle is suspect. If the oil pressure drops significantly as the engine warms up, the cause is most likely a very worn engine which is not going to go much farther without major problems.

If this low oil-pressure phenomenon shows up in a fairly low mileage car, it could be simply a faulty sending unit, or it could be wear, particularly if the car had been abused and rarely serviced. In any event, low or erratic oil pressure is a good reason to reject the car.

The temperature should remain constant even during hill climbing and stop and go driving. Many temperature related problems can be traced to a faulty thermostat or cooling fan switch. If the temperature never comes up to normal, the cause is most likely a thermostat that is stuck open, or a missing thermostat.

The cheapest fix for a bad thermostat is to remove it. The only problem is that the engine will never come up to normal operating temperature, and the temperature will not be stabilized under varying loads. A clear symptom of this problem is a heater which will not produce warm air.

A stuck-shut thermostat will cause the engine to overheat. It is unlikely that anyone will offer a car in this condition for sale, because a stuck-shut thermostat will cause the engine to overheat almost immediately. As soon as the engine is started, the temperature will just start climbing and climbing until the coolant boils.

If the engine seems to heat up too easily, like when climbing steep, long hills or idling in traffic, the problem is elsewhere and is reason enough to reject the car.

Another common cause for late- model cars to heat up while idling or poking along in traffic is that the electric cooling fan doesn't come on when it is supposed to. This can be the result of a bad temperature switch in the radiator, a faulty fan motor, or the repairman having inadvertently unplugged the connection while performing a non-related repair or service.

When the radiator is cool enough to remove the cap safely, look in and see what the coolant looks like. It should be bright and clear, the color of new coolant. If it looks black or brown, or the bottom of the radiator cap is covered with a greasy, dark film, look out. This is a strong symptom of combustion products in the coolant. The only way combustion products can get into the coolant is with a blown head gasket or a crack in the block or head. Yucky looking coolant is another reason to disqualify a car.

Unfortunately, a cooling-system problem can be easily hidden from view by simply cleaning or replacing the radiator cap and wiping the gunge from the inside of the radiator filler neck. If you have any reason to suspect that a problem exists, it would be wise to take the inspection one step further: stick your finger down into the radiator and take a sample from the inside of the radiator tank. Just reach in as far as you can, and rub your fingertip around wherever you can reach. Your finger should show only nice, clean coolant. There should be no dark-colored, greasy stuff. There is no reason for a healthy engine ever to have any oily or sooty deposits in its cooling system.

Another place to look for cooling-system gunge is in the plastic radiator overflow tank present on many cars. This tank receives the excess coolant as it expands from being heated by the engine. Then as the engine cools, the coolant returns to the radiator, thus keeping the radiator full at all times.

Incidentally, when checking the coolant level in a car not equipped with such a tank, the cold coolant level is normally a couple inches below the top. This allows for the expansion of the coolant as the engine comes up to temperature.

Let's move on to the automatic transmission. Pull out the transmission dipstick and inspect the fluid. On rear-wheel-drive cars, it will be located near the firewall. On front-wheel-drives, it is near the front of the engine compartment close to where the engine connects to the transmission. The transmission fluid should be transparent and pink with no brown tinge or opaqueness. Sniffing the end of the dipstick should reveal a sweet odor. If the fluid has even the slightest hint of burnt smell, and/or the color is anything but transparent pink/red, the transmission is worn past the limits of any possible adjustments and is guaranteed to fail shortly.

If your dream car proves to be a "10" in every respect except for its dubious transmission, buy it only if you can get a discount in the amount of a replacement transmission. And don't take the seller's word for how much that will be!

On front-wheel-drive autos and on the small four-wheel-drive units, the drive shafts which connect the trans-axle and differential to the wheels have constant velocity universal joints on each end. These CV joints are both extremely expensive and prone to early failure.

The biggest reason for premature failure is a break in the protective rubber boot which covers the joint. The grease runs out; water, snow and slush get in, and the precision-machined internal parts fail quickly. Boots often get injured by something as simple as stones kicked up from the road by the wheels, so periodic inspection is more than just a good idea.

Once you get into your test drive, there are some simple tests which will make a defective CV joint speak to you. Find a place to make some sharp, slow-speed turns. Parking lots work fine for this. Turn the wheel all the way to one side, and in a low gear at very low speed, step on the gas fairly hard for a moment, and listen. Now turn to the opposite side and repeat the operation. What you're supposed to hear is nothing.

If you hear a "click-click-click" noise, or something similar, one of the CV joints is going out on the side to which you were turning. This test will identify defective CV joints on either end of a four-wheel-drive.

Another test which will also find defective CV joints on both ends of most four-wheel drive, is a hard stop. This is best done if you can find a short, steep hill to go down, so that you will have more time to listen for noises. Get the car going 20 miles per hour or so, and then brake fairly hard, but not quite hard enough to stop the car before you get to the bottom of the hill. The same "click-click-click" noise will tell you of a defective CV joint.

Unless a boot has been broken or torn, CV joints on most cars don't generally become a problem before 70-80,000 miles. But it's important to find the defective ones in your prospective purchase, because the repairs are spendy. In some cars, the entire shaft assembly with both joints must be replaced, and they cost in the $300-500 range each!

After the engine is thoroughly warmed, and with the car parked, rev it up a few times and observe the exhaust. This is best accomplished with someone else doing the revving so that you can be behind the car to make your observation. By revving, we mean to punch the gas pedal a few times enough to really speed up the engine, but not to excess. There should be absolutely no smoke whatsoever.

If the engine is indeed thoroughly warmed up, as after your test drive, there should be no sign of moisture, either. No water in the tailpipe nor little droplets falling or blowing out.

Shut the engine off, and remove the oil filler cap. It should be reasonably clean and free from any sign of moisture. The bottom of the oil filler cap will be oily, but the oil should look like oil, not tar.

Checking the condition of the hoses and belts can tell what kind of maintenance the car has been receiving. No car owner who is conscientious about the care of his vehicle will allow belts to get old enough to start fraying or cracking. Radiator and heater hoses should be supple and free from cracks and bulgy spots.

If the car you are interested in is more than three years old, the belts and hoses should have been replaced by now. Replacement hoses can generally be spotted by new hose clamps which don't match the originals.

Another revealing test is to remove the top of the air cleaner. The paper replacement element should be reasonably clean and in good condition. The inside of the air-cleaner housing should also be clean. If there is any oil in here, look out. The engine either has a lot of blow by, which indicates badly worn piston rings, or there are some problems with the anti-pollution system.

The solution could be as simple as replacing a defective positive crankcase ventilation (PCV) valve, but it could also be a signal of serious problems. The advice of a competent mechanic is in order here.

A hoist is a valuable aid in checking out a car. Of course, the problem here is finding a mechanic with a hoist. It used to be that all service stations had hoists. But that was when we still had service stations.

(Now, in the interests of bottom-line accounting principles, we have mini-mart junk-food stores which sell gas as a sideline, and make you walk into the store to pay for the gas in an effort to expose you to their irresistible array of overpriced offerings. But we digress.)

From underneath, you will be able to see symptoms of many problems that the usual steam cleaning job will erase from view if your inspections are limited to under-hood.

Once you do get your prospective auto up on a

hoist, inspect the bottom of the engine for evidence of oil leaking from the front seal. This would show up in the form of a buildup of oily sludge on the bottom of the oil pan and surrounding components. In a severe case of any kind of an oil leak, there might even be shiny metal, kept clean by the continuous flow of oil.

Other specific areas to check for leaks are the fuel and oil pumps, transmission and torque-converter, power steering pump and hoses, trans-mission cooler plumbing, and the seals on tie-rod ends and other steering and suspension components. Check also for leaking shock absorbers and evidence of brake cylinder leaks. If you see any evidence of leaks anywhere, ask your mechanic to explain their source and implications for future problems.

Universal joints and half-shaft CV joints can also be easily inspected while the car is raised on a hoist. If at all possible, have someone knowledgeable in auto body repair check the frame and inner-panels for evidence of collision repairs.

One more check your mechanic can make while the car is in the air is for front-suspension and ball-joint wear. This is especially important on a car with over about 50,000 miles on it. Front suspension wear is directly proportional to the kinds of roads the car has been driven on for most of its life. Some 50,000 mile cars will have suspension components worn to the point where a proper front-end alignment is no longer possible, and others will be in near-perfect condition. Front end repairs are expensive. An overhaul can cost $300-600, depend-ing on the car.

So where do you look for a competent mechanic

to help you wade through the morass of the auto market? ASK FOR REFERRALS.

Ask as many people as you can, and when the same name starts coming up again and again, that's your mechanic. A super mechanic knows what's wrong with a car before it rolls to a stop in front of his shop. He diagnoses problems using his vast expertise and common sense, as opposed to the mechanic in an average franchised dealer's shop, who likely just starts replacing parts (at your expense) until he accidentally fixes the problem.

There is no substitute for expertise. A good mechanic, one who is also a good diagnostician, is a problem solver far superior to a bunch of dimwits in possession of a whole shop full of impressive diagnostic equipment. We've heard some pretty outrageous stories about the incompetence of "technicians" at so called diagnostic centers, as well as tales of several centers giving conflicting reports on the same problem.

Case in point: when our daughter was 21, she called to say she was going to drive the 500 miles to come for a visit. Because her car seemed to be using a little more gas than normal, she said that she would take it in to a nearby shop for a checkup before leaving. The shop, she said, looked impressive: lots of new, expensive cars and flashy looking equipment.

She took her car in, and the results of her checkup told her that her car needed a new oxygen sensor in the catalytic converter. It would cost about $125, but if she was "dumb enough to drive the car home the way it was, . . . [they] couldn't guarantee that it wouldn't catch on fire!" Our daughter called us first. We asked her if the "ECS" light on her dashboard was on. It wasn't. Aside from excessive gas consumption, the car was running just fine.

Since it was highly unlikely that her fairly-new, 30,000-mile car really needed an oxygen sensor, we advised her to drive the car up for her visit, that we would check it out when she got here. Even if it needed an oxygen sensor, the car would run just fine if possibly a trifle rich.

The problem? The automatic choke was not opening fully. The oxygen sensor checked out within factory tolerances. And an inexpensive voltmeter was all that was required to determine it, too.

Had our daughter listened to the high-pressure sales tactics of her garage mechanic, she would have been sold a $125 job which was unnecessary and her car still would not have been repaired. Unfortunately, this sort of incompetence and/or dishonesty is pervasive.

Many people labor under the delusion that if they take their Chevy to the Chevy dealer, the Honda to the Honda dealer, they're safe with "factory-trained" mechanics.

Most new-car stores hire their mechanics out of the same union hall as does everyone else. The guy who services your Toyota in the Toyota dealer's shop might have been doing Fords last week. For the most part, the notion of factory-trained mechanics is a myth. And on top of that, dealership garages generally have the most expensive shop rates and parts prices.

In all fairness, there are some dealerships that take pride in their repair facilities and make certain that their staff is competent. There are even some which won't intentionally sell you unnecessary parts and service. They are rare, however, so unless you get abundant recommendations and referrals to a specific dealership, independent shops are the way to go.

16. THE TEST DRIVE

Tell the seller that you wish to do a real test
drive, not a drive around the block. You
want to take the car out on the highway, up
and down some hills, let it poke along in
traffic, and then you want to find a big parking lot
to check out the CV joints (if applicable).

Then take a real test drive.

Observe how the car behaves before the engine is
fully warmed up. It should accelerate smoothly
from a stop. If it has a standard shift, there should be
no bucking and jerking when you let out the clutch.

Assuming the car has a carbureted engine, if it
either accelerates roughly or hesitates on shifting,
but seems to smooth out after the car is warmed up
to normal operating temperature, there is possibly a
problem in the automatic choke.

If the cold engine persists in running rough at any
low-power throttle setting, but smoothes out when

you step on the gas a little harder, the problem is probably in the carburetor itself. It probably needs to be disassembled and cleaned.

Take the car out on the freeway. Get it up to the speed you normally drive, a little higher would be better. Maintain speed for a while and pay attention to vibrations. Does the steering wheel shake a little?

A slight vibration in the wheel is a likely indication of out-of-balance tires, or perhaps just one tire. If the car appears to have nearly new tires, and the price of the car reflects the value of these tires, have the wheels balanced and try another highway run. If the problem persists, assume that at least one of the tires is defective, cannot be balanced, and must be replaced.

We recently bought a car at an auction after having thoroughly checked it out as far as we could. The test tracks at most auctions aren't long enough to allow the car to reach 50 miles per hour before it's time to jump on the brakes. This little beauty drove like new on its brand new set of tires.

As we left the auction, we took it out on the freeway. At 50 mph, the car started to rumble. At 55 it began to shake. At 60 it rumbled, shook, and roared. It was awful. And all that was wrong with it was those new tires.

Upon closer inspection, we noticed that there was no brand name, nor even the suggestion of a manufacturer on the tires. They were rejects that the seller knew were substandard. But he also knew that the buyer, a fellow dealer in this case, wouldn't find out until the car was paid for and out on the road.

If the road is level, hold the wheel very lightly and watch for any tendency to pull to one side or the other. If the road is crowned off to the right, as many are, there will be a slight tendency for the car to favor the right side of the road. This is normal, particularly with rack and pinion steering.

If you get a chance to drive the car on a road which is crowned to the left, however, the car should then exhibit an equal tendency to pull to the left. If the car exhibits abnormal tendencies, suspect a problem in the front suspension.

Find a road with very little traffic to test the brakes. At 30 or 40 mph, when you look in your mirror and see no vehicles close behind you, then press on the brake pedal hard enough to effect a serious stop, but not hard enough to skid (warn your passenger(s) of your intentions). This test works best going down a fairly steep hill.

No amount of braking should lock up any one wheel. If a wheel does lock up, suspect a leaky wheel cylinder, defective caliper, or a leaky bearing seal which is allowing grease to get on the linings or pads.

There must be no pull to either side. The car should stop perfectly straight. You should feel no vibration in the brake pedal. A hard, constant brake application at 30 to 40 miles per hour will demonstrate warped brake rotors with a firm pulsation you can feel in the brake pedal. Depending on how bad they are, the pulsation may continue until the car comes to a stop. Warped brake rotors are a result of overheating the brakes, which can be done in a number of ways, the most common of which is "riding" them.

Some people have the bad habit of constantly using their right foot on the gas and their left foot on the brakes. We have followed drivers for miles and observed that their brake lights go off only rarely.

Another bad habit is riding the brakes to coast down a long, fairly steep hill instead of shifting down to employ engine compression for the necessary braking effect. This is pure torture to the brakes. In any kind of normal driving, if you ever find yourself with your foot on the brake pedal for more than a few seconds at a time, you're doing something wrong.

In the interests of making your brake linings last their normal lifetime, use the technique of "fanning" your brakes. When you find the need to use your brakes for any extended period, do so in intervals, a few seconds on and a few seconds off. Do not use a steady, continued pressure.

If you discover warped brake rotors on your prospective purchase, have the seller agree to repair the problem. If the rotors are still repairable, the cost to do the front brakes would be in the neighborhood of $100 to $150. If the rotors need to be replaced, you're looking at a sizeable chunk of money. If he will agree, get him to pay to have the job done at the shop of your choice. And always get promises in writing. Remember, the seller is not legally liable for any verbal agreements.

If the seller does agree to repair the brakes, determine who is going to do the work, and check with the mechanic to make sure that the rotors are not being machined down past their safe limits.

With the car parked and the engine at idle, turn the steering wheel a full turn to one side and then to the other. (This test applies only if the car has power steering.) The wheel should turn smoothly with no jumping or intermittent hesitations. If you feel a kind of intermittent resistance to your turning effort, make sure that the air-conditioning is off to insure a normal idle speed. If that doesn't smooth it out, you are probably dealing with a fairly tired car, or at least one with some tired front suspension and/ or steering components. A mechanical checkup in this area is in order.

Now let's check the automatic transmission. From a full stop, accelerate at moderate throttle to about 35 miles per hour while paying close attention to shifting. The shifts should be very smooth, yet positive. You should not hear the engine revving even slightly as a shift occurs, and there should be no sign of "clunking" into gear on either up or down shifts.

If the speeds at which the automatic transmission shifts gears, or anything else about it seems unusual to you, consult your mechanic for an opinion.

You're looking at a five-speed? First, see how the clutch works.

Before you take off, check the free play of the clutch pedal. You should be able to press the clutch pedal down very lightly with your fingertips and feel (depending on make and model) from a half-inch to a little over an inch of "play" (free travel) before the pedal comes in contact with the clutch mechanism. It's hard to describe in words, but you'll know what it is when you feel it.

The reason for this check is to determine whether or not the clutch is in proper adjustment. If it is correctly adjusted, there will be the proper amount of free play. If there is no free play, or if the pedal moves several inches before engaging the clutch, it is out of adjustment. It is difficult to determine the condition of the clutch itself when it is out of adjustment.

A poorly adjusted clutch pedal is highly suspect in a car for sale. It means either the car has been poorly serviced (clutch adjustments are part of proper periodic maintenance), or that the clutch linkage has been deliberately mal-adjusted to disguise a worn-out clutch.

When you let out the clutch, it must engage smoothly and positively. The clutch should start to engage when it is about half way up from the floor. Closer to the floor is OK, but much more than half way up speaks of a worn clutch which may need replacement soon. Any shuddering or vibration felt upon clutch engagement means replacement is on the near horizon.

When cruising along in fourth gear at about 25 or 30 miles per hour on level ground and while maintaining a light throttle, push the clutch in very lightly for just a brief moment and then let it right back out. It should re-engage firmly and with no perceptible increase in engine speed. If the re-engagement results in much engine speed up and/or feels mushy when it re-engages, the clutch might well be worn out. If you have any doubts about the results of this test, make a note of it on the checklist for your mechanic.

The weakest parts of most manual transmissions are the synchronizers, or "synchros". The synchros instantly adjust the speeds of the gears as you shift, to enable the individual gears to mesh without grinding. If a transmission has been abused by hard shifting, the synchros wear out prematurely, and make it difficult to shift without grinding the gears. The best way to check for worn synchros is to do exactly what you're not supposed to do: shift fast and hard.

Just this one time, pretend you are on a race track. Accelerate to get to 60 miles per hour as if your life depends on it. Shift quickly and firmly. The shifts should be smooth and quiet. Full throttle acceleration is not necessary, but the quick, firm shifts are. Any grinding noise as you shift into the next gear means shot synchros, and shot synchros only get worse. If you can make them misbehave with this test, it won't be too long before you notice the grinding during normal shifting.

One more test: when you get into top gear, shift back down, quickly and firmly, through each gear as you bring the car back to a stop. Again, the shifts should be smooth and quiet. You will likely feel some resistance in the shift lever on down shifting, particularly if done at higher speeds than those at which you normally shift. This resistance is the synchros doing their job. This is not a good practice to do every time you shift down, but just this once it's OK. Shifts should, at all times, be smooth and quiet.

Out of habit, we really take it easy on our cars. We have bought a few cars with edgy transmissions just because we resist "speed shifting" during a test drive. But experience has taught us to shift up and down through all the gears, hard and fast, while test driving any car. Any gear crunching on a hard shift means that at least one previous owner made a habit of that kind of shifting, and unless you're prepared to repair the transmission, you don't want the car.

A note on down shifting: many people seem to think that they should shift down through each gear every time they come to a stop. Continual down-shifting is the kiss of death to transmission synchros. Generally, the only time necessary to down-shift is when approaching a long downhill stretch where you will need compression to avoid riding the brakes. In average driving situations, the proper way to come to a stop is to anticipate the stop early, take your foot off the gas to allow the car to decelerate so that a light braking will bring you to a stop.

Brakes last a long time and are fairly inexpensive to reline. Transmissions are real spendy to fix. To shift down through each gear every time you come to a stop is putting a lot of unnecessary wear on your transmission, not to mention your arm.

17. WHAT TO DO WHEN IT BREAKS

An automobile is an incredibly complex machine. It is actually a combination of many complex individual machines, each of which must perform perfectly all the time, under all conditions, with anyone at all operating the controls. It is not surprising then, especially considering the abuse that many cars must endure, that some parts of these wonderful machines occasionally malfunction.

Most machinery, whether it is in a big factory or in your home workshop, comes with very complete operating instructions. Even fairly simple, single-purpose equipment is supplied with instructions and many cautions, reminding the operator of what can go wrong if the rules aren't strictly adhered to.

Not so with an automobile. There can be no rules because nobody would read them. (When is the last time you read an automobile owner's manual?)

Here is one of the most complex pieces of machinery commonly available, certainly the most complex available to the general public, and it has to be designed to be foolproof.

It has to do its thing exactly the same way for an experienced, careful operator, as for someone who has never driven a car before. It has to work perfectly for operators who have not the foggiest notion of what makes it all happen. And as our cars grow ever more complicated, more and more devices need to be engineered and installed so that the whole package will still be idiot proof.

The folks who trade in their cars for new ones every year or two probably never have to deal with the possibility of a major repair. Were they to do an objective analysis of the costs of this luxury, they would no doubt be astonished.

You, on the other hand, have not allowed yourself to be lured into this kind of extravagance. You decided long ago to get your money's worth out of your automobile, right? And you may get through your entire life without having to face the ultimate repair job: an engine replacement. But then, maybe not.

What do you do when your trusted diagnostician says that you need a new engine? The first thing almost everyone does is start pricing overhauled engines. Some people even go to their new-car dealer and price a brand new engine.

Neither of these is the most cost-effective alternative.

Let's see how your car came to need a new engine in the first place. The car has likely been driven over 100,000 miles, and the engine is just plain worn out. There are hundreds of wearing parts in your engine. And when they are almost all worn to the same degree, it makes no sense to do a band-aid repair: fixing just the worst-worn parts.

There are lots of repair shop owners/managers who will gladly take in your car when you complain of some specific problem, for example, excessive oil consumption. They'll tell you that they can just put in a new set of rings and you will get another 50,000 miles out of the old engine.

But as soon as your car is in his shop with its engine mostly disassembled, you will, quite predictably, get a phone call. The garage keeper will explain to you that, upon inspecting the innards of your engine, he found that the engine really does need a complete overhaul. He is sorry to have to tell you, of course, and he WOULD, as he promised you (to get your car in his shop), do just the rings, but he would not be able to guarantee his work.

This is one of the oldest sales gimmicks in the repair business. First, you are told that you don't need the expensive repair that someone else said you needed. That line gets your attention right away. Then you get a promise of how the band-aid repair will save you a bunch of money. Now you're hooked. You turn over the keys, and you have just gone down with the sinker.

You will get the phone call, and the price of a "proper" repair job will probably end up costing you more than the original quote for an overhaul. The mechanic will cover himself by explaining to you that he will honor his original repair estimate, but he will also plant the seeds of doubt in your mind by telling you that he certainly couldn't guarantee his work if you chose not to do the job right.

He has effectively washed his hands of the whole affair, and it has suddenly become your problem. He also has your car disassembled in his shop. You will pay his price, the price he knew in the beginning he would get.

Almost any time a mechanic tells you that he can do a fairly major repair on a tired, high-mile engine in order to save you the cost of a complete overhaul, you are probably being set up to pay the price of a complete overhaul, and then some. The irony of the whole thing is that most repair shops are not equipped to do overhauls properly anyway, so even after you end up paying through the nose to get your car back, it still won't be right.

In our 30+ years in the car business, we have dealt with a large number of "overhauled" engines. We have never seen an overhauled engine which we would have wanted in our own car.

The words "overhaul" and "rebuild" mean different things to different people. To some low-life mechanics, a reasonably quiet used engine or transmission with a thorough steam cleaning and a fresh coat of paint qualifies as rebuilt.

Most reputable shops do not do their own overhauls. They buy "exchange overhaul" engine blocks from a large rebuild shop that does nothing but rebuild engines. They install one of these engine blocks in your car. Your old block then goes back to the rebuild shop as a core for another rebuild.

Rebuild shops, as every other business, come with varying degrees of integrity. Here's an example of what you might buy from one of the better rebuild shops.

Every part in an engine has a dimensional tolerance.

Dimensional tolerances, or size limits, are the parameters set for gauging worn parts. If the wear exceeds the dimensional tolerances, the parts in question must be replaced. If a main bearing journal, for example, is supposed to be 3" in diameter, but is allowed a wear tolerance of .003" before a replacement is called for, the shop may with a clear conscience, reuse a crankshaft that measures .00299" undersize. It is, as they say, within tolerance.

So the rebuilt engine you buy might just have a crankshaft installed with its bearing journals so close to the edge of the wear tolerance that in another few thousand miles of normal use, it will be worn beyond that tolerance, or according to the manufacturer's specifications, worn out. The same conditions apply to every moving part in the engine.

A freshly overhauled engine, therefore, can conceivably be almost worn out when you get it. In just a few thousand miles, an engine with parts barely within tolerances could well be in worse shape than it was before you had it overhauled. There are some rebuilders who guarantee that certain parts are always replaced with new ones, and they will furnish you a list of these parts. But even then, the new parts are usually aftermarket. Aftermarket parts are those made by someone other than the manufacturer of the original equipment.

A factory assembly line is much better able to produce consistently high quality engines than is any repair shop which has to make the many compromises necessary to enable it to handle hundreds of different makes and models.

In all fairness, we have to say that somewhere out there, there might be an engine rebuilder who does a decent job. It's just that we have never been able to find him, and we've looked, too. We've had rebuilt engines from sources ranging from cheapo mass production rebuild factories to independent machine shops of high repute.

The information presented here is derived from experience with overhauled engines in cars that we have bought, taken in trade, or been associated with for other reasons. It also comes from stories told to us by friends, relatives, business associates and customers. Based on all this input, it seems safe to say that it is always a big gamble to have any major repairs done to an aging engine.

Even one of the better rebuilt engines will rarely make it past 50,000 miles before it starts to blow smoke and develop funny noises. We have known very few overhauled engines which didn't make funny noises right out of the box. Lifter noises, timing chain rattles, piston slap, wrist pin rattles, you name it. Yet often, these engines fresh from the rebuilder that sounded pretty awful to us, didn't sound unusual to their owners at all. That must be why rebuilders get away with selling all those edgy engines. People either don't know any better, or they just don't care.

Lots of owners of rebuilt engines have complained about excessive oil consumption and exhaust smoke right from the beginning. The garage usually gives the same stock answer: "We use such high quality rings in our engines that they take longer to seat than ordinary rings. The engine will smoke and use oil for a while, and that's normal. Just ignore it for now, and when those rings seat, the engine will be better than new."

What is really being said is that you should just live with it until the warranty runs out, at which time it's your problem. An engine that smokes excessively when new will probably always smoke.

So you forget about rebuilt engines and see about a brand new one from the dealer. OK, the car has a little over 100,000 miles on it. The engine is getting noisy, doesn't always start like it used to, and it is using oil. The blue haze coming from the exhaust can no longer be ignored. You go to the dealer.

After recovering from the shock that the new engine will cost over $2,000 installed (in many cases more than the car is worth), you ask just what you will get for the money. You are told that you get a factory new block and heads: the entire engine, minus the carburetor or fuel injection, distributor, and accessories.

The accessories include all the emission-control hardware, alternator, air-conditioning compressor, belts, and in some cases, the water pump. You sign the order and the work begins. A few days later, you pick up your car, and after writing the big check, you drive it home. You notice that it still has that same funny hesitation upon acceleration.

The next morning you notice that it still doesn't start like it ought to, and on the way to work, you stop at the dealer's. He tells you that those little glitches are in the carburetor, which as you know, has over 100,000 miles on it and really ought to be replaced. So, $300 later, you drive off again, only to have the 100,000 mile, $140 alternator go belly up.

And as soon as the hot days of summer are upon you, the 100,000 mile air-conditioning compressor goes out. Not to mention the old, tired emission-control hardware, which only causes occasional minor problems.

So, what is the solution? Remember way back when your car had only 50,000 miles on it? Remember how well it ran then, how dependable it was? Suppose that your car had been involved in an accident then. Someone had run into the back of it and damaged it beyond repair. The body was damaged beyond repair, but the engine wasn't even touched.

Right now, today, in an auto salvage yard near you, there is a low-mileage engine that came out of a car identical to yours. The car was involved in an accident, but the engine came out unhurt.

That engine can be bought for about one-third the price of an overhaul. And at that low price, it will include the carburetor, alternator and all of the usual accessories. All those external parts and accessories will also be low-mileage. And since the engine is a complete assembly, your mechanic will be able to install it in a fraction of the time for a fraction of the cost that it would take to install a rebuilt or new block using all of your old, worn out externals.

We will take our chances on just about any reasonably well-maintained 50,000 mile factory engine over any newly rebuilt engine. A new factory engine might outlast the used one, but consider the price of the new engine, and remember your eventual need to replace all of the expensive external parts.

Any time you are told that your aging auto needs a repair as major as a valve job, or anything else requiring a fairly substantial disassembly of the engine, you would probably be better off to replace the entire engine with a good, low-mileage used one.

Do not be intimidated by the words "wrecking yard." For the most part, there are no more wrecking yards. No more wading through ankle deep grease to get to the filthy counter in a dingy little shack out in the middle of a sea of overturned, smashed cars. Nowadays you go to "auto parts recyclers." And the difference goes far beyond the name. Most of these businesses are expertly managed, carefully controlled operations with clean showrooms and computer managed inventories.

At most inner-city dismantler's businesses, you won't even see any wrecked cars, just a well run parts store. To purchase an engine from a recycler, you need only go to the one nearest you. If he doesn't have the exact number you need, he'll find it quickly on his "hot-line". All of the parts recyclers are inter-connected on one or more hot-lines and cooperate with one another in locating parts.

You could, of course, get on the phone and call around to the various businesses until you locate the right engine yourself. For any 1980 or newer engine, you should find a replacement of the same model year to insure that the emission control hardware will hook up directly. A different year engine might be basically identical and actually bolt up to your transmission, but if the emission control plumbing is even a little bit different, your mechanic might spend hours trying to make it work. Or worse yet, he might do his best and still not get it to pass inspection.

Once you have located the correct engine, tell the salesperson that you want to look at the car it came out of. There is a good chance that the car in question is no longer in the yard. It has probably already been completely scavenged for useful parts and the rest sent to the crusher.

But if possible, examine the car. Check the odometer, if it is still there. Look over the interior, and try to determine whether the car appears to have been taken care of. You'll have to ignore the damage caused by the wreck, of course, but usually it is apparent even in a wreck, if a car has been abused. An abused body and interior is a pretty good indicator of the care received by the engine.

Look on the upper left corner of the windshield or the end of the driver's door (assuming that the car has a windshield and/or a driver's door) for lube stickers which can give clues to whether or not the engine was serviced properly. If you are lucky, you might even locate an engine which hasn't yet been removed from the car. Then you will have the opportunity to inspect the engine for oil leaks and general outside condition. When engines are pulled, they generally get steam cleaned, effectively removing any evidence of leaks.

The engine should look about like yours did with the same number of miles on it. The whole engine compartment should have about the same level of griminess, with no buildups of grease or visible evidence of oil leaks. There must be no rust stains which would show that the radiator had at one time boiled over. Never consider an engine if there is any evidence that it has ever been overheated.

Check the inside of the radiator, or if it has already been removed, the inside of a radiator hose or hose fitting on the engine. It should be sparkling clean. There must be no evidence of oil, rust, or sooty black deposit.

Check the oil, breather cap, air filter element just as if you were checking out a used car for possible purchase. Look for lube stickers. Look in the glove box for repair receipts. Sometimes you can find entire repair histories in glove boxes of wrecks in auto-salvage yards.

What about exchangeability; the possibility of using an engine other than the exact make and model being replaced? As mentioned earlier, changing non-exact engines in cars newer than about 1980 is generally risky because of the emission control hardware. There are federal laws prohibiting the alteration of this hardware, which makes the situation stickier yet.

Engines lacking the same emissions control hardware can be exchanged using your old hardware, but this often means using your old carburetor or fuel injection and even the intake manifold. A consultation with the person who will do the work is in order here. Given the right price for the engine, it might be worth while.

But don't give up too easily finding the correct replacement. There are so many cars in these yards, mostly late-model units, that the selection is amazing. And with the industry's practice of using the identical car in several model lines, such as Chevy Celebrity, Pontiac J-6000, Buick Century and Olds Ciera, the selection gets even better because an Olds Ciera engine can be a direct replacement for a same year Pontiac J-6000, etc. The same thing goes for most other domestic marques, too.

There is also a real market for other-than-exact engine replacements. Any older car qualifies, and the big market is for special interest cars. These can include those which are of special interest to you only, as well as cars of great value. (See Chapter 13.)

For example, say you have found an exceptionally nice 1966 Chevy Impala. You like the car a lot, and everything about it is great except that it has 43,000 miles on the odometer, which you can see means at least 143,000 miles, and the engine is tired. Any small block Chevrolet from a great range of years will bolt directly into this chassis.

If you want to retain your original distributor instead of the electronic ignition of newer engines, it is directly replaceable, too. The possibilities of shuffling around engines, manifolds, carburetors and even transmissions on these older cars are endless. Many GM cars used the same engines for years, and they are directly interchangeable.

If you find an older car in great shape but you aren't crazy about the zillion horsepower, gas guzzling engine, be comforted to know that most of these engines can be exchanged for the smaller, more efficient engines available for the car when it was new. Your local auto dismantler/recycler has "interchange manuals" which tell exactly which engines will exchange directly with which others.

Often employees at auto recyclers can tell you which engines will exchange by making a few simple adjustments or by installing both engine and transmission as a unit. Many older cars will accept a newer engine in every hookup except to the transmission. Assuming the car is worth spending the money, installing an engine/transmission assembly might solve the problem and give you a fresh transmission in the bargain.

Engines and transmissions are not the only parts which are often better purchased used. Ever wait too long to do a brake reline and have to buy new rotors or drums? Ouch! Used, they are available for about one-third the price of new ones. It is good practice to consider your auto dismantler first whenever you need parts.

Glass is another good example. If you ever had the misfortune to break any uninsured auto glass and had to pay for it yourself, you know all about it. A door window for a bottom-of-the-line import can cost several hundred dollars. Without getting into the insanities of this kind of pricing, let's just say that a replacement can be purchased at a dismantler for about one-third of the new price, often even less.

Even if you don't do your own repairs, you can ask your repair person to inquire about used parts first before buying any new ones. Used parts are usually just a phone call away from your mechanic's place of business. Most salvage yards will deliver parts to local repair shops.

Not all repairs will call for something as serious as an engine overhaul. More often than not, when a car breaks down, the problem is minor. Too often, because there are very few mechanics capable of accurate problem diagnoses, minor problems turn into expensive, if not unnecessary, repairs.

Building intelligent consumers is what this book is all about. Some of the scams pulled on car owners by larcenous repair facilities are hard to believe. And almost all of them would be impossible to pull off if the car owner had even the most cursory knowledge of what made his car run.

If you just don't want to be bothered to learn

anything about your vehicle and how it works, you still have the means to avoid the rip-off artist. Get a second opinion or better yet a third. You will be surprised at the different diagnoses of the same problem you will get if you present it to several different mechanics.

In many cases, garages have specialty areas in which they abuse their customer's confidences. For example, some mechanics will sell you a battery no matter what is wrong with your car. Even if you leave it for an oil change, they'll at least try to sell you that battery.

Some will just try a verbal approach, implying that your present battery is on its last leg and might at any time leave you stranded, and that you really ought to take advantage of this opportunity to buy a battery at the "sale" price instead of waiting until you're stuck on the freeway in the middle of the night in a rainstorm.

Others use a more aggressive approach. You leave your car for an oil change or some other service, and a couple of hours later you return to pick it up. While paying the bill, the manager informs you that he had to jump-start your car to pull it into the shop and that you must have a bad battery. You tell him that the battery is only a year old and you've never had any problem with it. He says, well then it's probably shorted out. That can happen at any time with no warning. Let's go check it out.

You follow him to the car, and he uses his battery tester to show you how the battery is indeed nearly dead. Shorted cell, he says, and boy are you ever in luck. He's running a battery sale right now and he can let you have a brand new battery for only $49.95, installed. He could, of course just charge up your old battery and you could maybe get by for a few more days . . . .

What happened? When you left your car, the mechanic put a big load on your battery to make sure that if you tried to start the car, it wouldn't. He's really good at this trick, having perfected it during the last ten years.

Our daughter recently took her car to a state-certified pollution control inspection station for a mandatory inspection. The inspection cost her $36, and what she got for her money was a printout informing her that $90 worth of work was required to get the car to pass. After the $90 worth of work was completed, she would have to pay another $36 inspection fee, and then another $6 for the certificate she would need to present to the motor vehicles department. She called home for advice.

We told her to write off the $36 to experience, ignore the advice she got for her money, and to try another inspection station, but first to ask around for referrals. It worked. The next place did the same inspection to the same car, using the same state-mandated performance specifications, and with the simple adjustment of the idle-speed screw on the carburetor, the car passed with flying colors. No repairs were needed.

She could have saved herself $36, an anxious phone call, and a lot of time by asking for referrals first. Had she elected to go with the advice of the first shop, she would have dropped $168 for a service which was overpriced at $36. Clearly, this is thievery.

Need more evidence? An auto dealer friend recently told of a late-model Chevy pickup that he bought at an auction. It ran fine under most conditions but would not idle smoothly. He sent it to the local Chevrolet dealer for the necessary repair. The repair bill from that dealer was nearly $600; he allegedly replaced almost every component in the engine's pollution-control systems. The engine ran a little more smoothly, but it still was not right. After a week, it ran as roughly as it did when the dealer bought it.

He then took it to a diagnostic clinic, where he was told that the engine "probably" needed a valve job. After the dealer's own mechanic did a compression check which indicated no need of a valve job, he sent the truck to yet one more garage, a small local shop where the owner had a reputation as a skillful diagnostician. He found and replaced a defective vacuum hose, which fixed the problem. The charge? $24 for labor and $1 for the hose.

Or try this one. Harold left his two-year-old, 18,000 mile Oldsmobile Regency at the body shop for a fender-bender repair. The shop owner had one just like it, only his had 95,000 miles on it. It still ran OK, but it was getting tired. After the shop closed for the night, he pulled Harold's car into the back room, removed the engine, and replaced it with the engine from his car. The body-repair job got done, and Harold picked up his car. Not until many months later did he start getting messages from his engine that it seemed to be wearing out prematurely. What really happened never occurred to him.

Sound preposterous? You bet, but it happens, and not only with engines.

Rather than devote this entire book to depressing case histories of auto-repair thievery, we suggest that you just consider your own past experiences with auto-repair facilities, and talk them over with any friend who owns a car. You are certain to hear as many horror stories as you have the time and patience for. Very unfortunately, this industry deserves all the bad press it gets, and then some.

In most states, the garages even have legal protection to conduct their thievery. A mechanic or garage can hold your car under a legal mechanic's lien until his bill is paid. If the bill gets disputed in court, he is the expert witness in his own behalf. After all, what do you know about it? You're just a consumer. And more than likely, so is the judge.

A word of advice: if you find that you have been unquestionably ripped off, do not stop payment on the check with which you paid the garage! File a claim in small-claims court to recover your money, but don't stop payment.

A stop payment can backfire to the point where the garage keeper ends up suing you, or at the very least, having your complaint dismissed. In most states a stop-payment is considered fraud. They assume that your intent was to make the garage keeper believe you were paying for a service you actually had no intention of paying.

Your best defense is to know your car at least well enough to be able to detect a repair diagnosis which is obviously wrong. Failing that, we recommend that you get at least two different opinions before signing the repair order.

This might make you want to run right down to your nearest diagnostic clinic, that fancy, computer-equipped facility which supports its claim to reputability by telling you that since it sells only diagnostic expertise and no parts or repairs, it is not likely to tell you of non-existent problems.

But problems do exist with the clinics. Again, this is a generalization based upon lots of our own experience and that of many customers, business associates, and friends. For all we know, there just might be a diagnostic clinic out there somewhere from which you could get some useful information.

It has been our experience that diagnostic clinics are quite capable of giving a "worn out" report on a brand new car. They can also overlook serious discrepancies, as well as give diagnoses inconsistent with other diagnostic centers and with reality. There is no substitute for a skilled, if hard-to-find human diagnostician.

The gentleman who did our mechanical work before we moved was a great diagnostician. He often knew exactly what was wrong with the car before it rolled to a stop in front of his shop. He knew automobiles inside and out. He never blindly replaced parts in an effort to discover which one was defective.

When you do finally decide on the shop that is going to repair your car, never leave the car until you have signed and received a copy of the repair order. Read the fine print. Make sure that the repair order doesn't have any loopholes which authorize the shop to do any work beyond what you authorized under any circumstances.

If the full price of the repair cannot be stated on the repair order, make certain that the order states that you will be notified of the price before the work is done. You may elect to put a dollar-ceiling on the work above which you must be notified before doing the job. Rest assured that that ceiling will be reached.

Make it known that you want to inspect both the removed parts and the packages which held the replacement parts. Unfortunately, some shops keep an inventory of damaged or worn parts just to have them on hand to show to people who insist on inspecting replaced parts. The parts you are shown may be from such an inventory.

Most auto-repair facilities today are parts replacing establishments. You bring in your car with a complaint of a specific problem, and the mechanic more or less blindly goes about replacing parts until, by accident, he eventually finds the one which was defective. Of course, you are charged for all of the parts, eventhough all but one were fine and didn't need replacement. And you are charged anywhere from $25 to $60 per hour for the mechanic's time.

Most of the electronic "black boxes" tucked away in all sorts of obscure places in our newer cars are a mystery to even the best repair specialists. If the shop's diagnostic computer detects a malfunction in one of the black boxes, the black box gets replaced. They are sealed units, designed to be discarded for any malfunction. There is no repair possible, and most are protected either physically or electroni-cally against any enterprising manufacturer dupli-cating them and selling them as aftermarket replacements for a reasonable price. Some of these little wonders cost several hundred dollars, and have about as much hardware tucked inside as a ten dollar radio.

Many of these black boxes are also unnecessarily hidden in inaccessible corners of the car, as inside a quarter-panel where several hours of shop time will be required to remove most of the car's interior just to get at the thing.

It's all part of modern merchandising. There is no legitimate reason for the astronomical prices of replacement auto parts.

There is no reason why a grille, made of cheap PVC plastic (the same stuff plastic water pipe is made of) and about as complex as a seventy-nine cent ice-cube tray, should cost the consumer $100.

There is no reason why a fender for a small import, a fender with as much metal in it as a $7.95 trash can, should cost the consumer $120. It isn't even galvanized!

Consider this: it used to be, you could buy a taillight lens for an average car for $15 or so, until modern merchandising practices.

The highly-paid executives who decide these practices determined that it was a shame the consumer could get by with having to pay only $15 for this lens, which was about as complicated as many $1.39 kids' toys. To solve this dilemma, they simply glued the lens onto the very expensive taillight housing, which included the lamp sockets, wiring harness, and reflectors, and sold the whole thing as a unit.

Now if you happen to crack your unnecessarily fragile taillight lens and go to the dealer for a replacement, you are told that this part is serviced only as a taillight unit, and you'll have to pay $135! Then, you get to throw the perfectly good original lamp housing, with all its perfectly good hardware, in the trash.

This practice is not limited to taillight assemblies; it is becoming pervasive throughout this industry and others. At a time when we are all striving to conserve resources, these industry leaders bow to the bottom line and create an ever increasing throw away society. Not only is this a grossly dishonorable business practice, it is environmentally obscene.

How do they get away with it?

First of all, we have proven again and again to the merchandising executives that we are a nation of sheep and we will hold still for just about anything that they tell us is acceptable.

Second, in almost all cases, who cares how much it costs to fix a car damaged in an accident? The insurance pays the bill, right? The consumer doesn't care. After all, with those high premiums that he has to pay, it serves the insurance company right to get nailed with a fat repair bill now and then. Guess why the insurance premiums are high.

We wonder if it isn't a big conspiracy. The consumers don't care what the repairs cost because the insurance company pays the repair bills. The insurance companies don't care how high the repair bills get because they just raise our premiums to whatever level it takes to maintain their enormous profits. The body shops love it, because their profit is directly proportional to the repair bill.

Overpriced replacement costs are not unique to body parts. Most mechanical repair parts have doubled in price over the last few years as well.

Aren't you curious about where all the extra money goes? Ask any parts store counter person if he has received a raise in the last few years, and you are likely to hear nothing but groans. Ask the owner of the store if his profit margin has been increased in the last few years. More groans. Ask the factory workers in the plants where the parts are manufactured about recent raises. Of course, you'll have to leave the country to get to many of the factories.

Ask anyone in the entire chain of command right from manufacturing down to the final retail sale. As in almost all areas of our economy, it is the few at the top who are siphoning the cream off the efforts of all the rest of us.

What can we do about it? Without getting politically involved up to our eyeballs, not much. We could stop buying new cars. That would be a viable, easily manageable, and very powerful statement to the auto industry. It is within our power as a nation of consumers to cease buying new cars until the automakers refrain from some of their more conscienceless practices and overpricing.

As long as we continue to accept the insane price increases, we will continue to get them. It would indeed be easy to let the automakers know that their bizillion dollar advertising campaigns no longer work, and that we're through being their suckers.

We can minimize the impact of this thievery in our own lives by become intelligent consumers. By not letting someone sell us something we don't need. By buying used whenever possible. By properly maintaining our cars so that they won't need replacement parts in the first place.

It is unfortunate that we have to go to such lengths to avoid getting taken by the unscrupulous people in the automobile industry. What is just as unfortunate is the unwarranted burden that this well-deserved reputation of deceit places on the few honest individuals trying to operate within the system. For them, it is truly demeaning to have everyone who comes through their doors view them as thieves and cheats.

Happily, the honest businessman seems to have no trouble attracting more word of mouth referrals than he can handle. It is our sincere recommendation that if you are lucky enough to be told by several sources of such a dealer or repairman, that you assume that he is honest and conduct your business with him accordingly.

18. CONCLUSION

Throughout this book, we have been consistent in our attempt to discourage you from considering the purchase of a new car. The reasons are simple, and the main reason is economics. Unless you have money to burn, it just doesn't make good sense to buy a new car. We have given you examples to ponder and numbers to compare your personal budget to the purchase of your next car.

Another reason for considering an older car is that in many ways, older cars are better than newer ones. This is, of course, a generalization. But consider the examples we have given.

Each new year, the automakers, in their never ending campaign to cheapen every detail, have given us less and charged us more. Each new year brings with it more complexity. Each complication lessens the likelihood of anyone other than an authorized dealer being able to diagnose, service, or repair our cars. Each new year, the automakers figure out more ways to use every transaction to rob us of more hard-earned dollars.

Yet another reason to stop buying new cars is to give a message to an industry that feels that the American public is indeed a flock of sheep. We must let them know that we will not pay any price for that which the advertising gods tell us we must have. For as long as we continue to pay more each year, we will continue to get higher prices.

Each year, cars become more insanely expensive. Just as the industry promised us 20 years ago, people are now paying over $20,000 for a new Honda, and loving it.

One way to have all of the thrill of new car ownership and never lose it is to find a special interest car in pristine condition and maintain it that way forever. Special interest cars never depreciate and are always worth repairing. Well-chosen special interest cars are excellent investments. Long after your neighbor's new-car buzz wears down, you will still be the proud owner of an exceptional, head-turning automobile.

Remember when a quality automobile was so quiet that you could scarcely hear it drive up? People are growing used to the cheap sounding, tinny noise of many of the new cars. Just as the industry expects us to, we are accepting everything they hand us. Ever notice the remarkable similarity between the sound of the engines in many of the new cars and your neighbor's kid's $300 Pinto? Yes, appearing somewhere in one of today's new cars is an embarrassment, not an exhilaration.

The auto industry's reputation as a den of thieves is well earned. Dealers are out to rip off their marks, other dealers, those who they sublet work to, and anyone else in their paths. They are taught to do this at highly charged, professionally prepared training seminars.

Dealerships juggle the sales figures to cheat their own salesmen out of fair commissions, the salesmen do their best to cheat on the house and on each other, and they're all out to cheat the public. From the highest level to the lowest, there is little honor.

By knowing how the industry trains its people to manipulate, misrepresent, and coerce, we can survive the ordeal they have made of buying a car. If we're up to it, we can even have fun beating them at their own games.

We will never under any circumstances talk "trades" with a dealer.

We will never even admit to currently owning a car. We will never discuss financing with a dealer.

We will always have our financing in the bag before we go shopping.

We can find the few honorable individuals who are, against the odds of the reputation imposed upon them by their less-than-honorable fellows, running reputable sales and repair organizations.

We can find a reputable and competent repairman who has both the diagnostic expertise and the equipment to keep our cars running at peak efficiency.

We can inspect a car offered for sale by a private-party, and know how to inspect the seller as well as the car.

At the very least, we can determine our automotive needs in an intelligent, objective manner, and find a car that is both a good value and a sound, safe ride.

We can do all this while neatly side-stepping the games dealers play.

INDEX

A

actual cash value (ACV) 39, 68-70, 85
adjuster 58-66
advertising 5, 10, 33, 119, 145, 154-156, 170, 187, 195
aerodynamic 121
aftermarket 59, 60, 62, 99, 180, 194
aftermarket parts 59, 60, 62, 180
air-conditioning 94, 97, 100, 101, 132, 139, 150, 154,
    172, 182
American cars 90
auctions 25, 31, 36, 37, 40, 41, 43-46, 83, 95, 120, 169
auto salvage 183
automatic transmission 94, 95, 104, 160, 172

B

bid, insurance 64, 65
Blue Book, the 35-39
body repair 59, 141, 164
body shop 61-64, 65, 141, 146, 147, 191, 196
book, the 35-39, 75, 95, 101
brakes 94, 95, 132, 170

C

car size 79, 119
cheap cars 109, 111
clutch 95, 96, 139, 149, 168, 172, 173
cold engine 153, 168
collision insurance 57, 86
collision repair 144, 164
comfort 26, 79, 80, 86, 96, 97, 100, 106, 108, 110,
    111, 119, 121, 131, 140, 149, 187
contracts 75
control 10, 12-15, 17, 18, 22
cooling system 103, 139, 160

credit limit 74
credit union 73, 74
cruise control 94, 96, 97
curbstoner 30-33
CV joint 161, 164, 168

D

dealers, shade-tree 31
decisions 6, 7, 10, 13, 39, 107
diagnostic clinic 165, 191-193
diesel 120
door locks, power 94, 97

E

economy car 104
engine 7, 54, 55, 79, 81-83, 90, 92-94, 101, 103,
     104, 116, 120, 121, 133-136, 139, 140, 142,
     152-160, 162-164, 168, 171-173, 177-188, 191, 200
engine overhaul 188
engine size 93
engine swap 133-135
estimates 64, 65
European car 92
examination 83, 138
exhaust 162, 181, 182
exotic car 78
expenses 42, 86, 108, 110

F

factory engine 183
Federal Trade Commission 47, 50
financing 73, 74, 105
FTC sticker 47-50, 55, 56
fuel mileage 9, 92-94
full-size cars 79, 119

G

gas mileage 11, 45, 79, 87, 89, 100, 101, 104, 108, 135
gears 84, 96, 172-174
guages 62, 74, 127

guarantees 33, 48, 160, 165, 178, 180

H

Hemmings Motor News 130, 135
high mileage 38

I

idiot lights 153-156
insurance 4, 31, 42-44, 48, 51-53, 57-66, 75, 78, 79, 86,
     105, 106, 140, 148, 196
insurance adjuster 60, 63
insurance company 42-44, 59-64, 148, 196
insurance salvage auction 31, 42
interior 90, 114, 117, 149, 150, 185, 195
inventory 17, 25, 27, 28, 41, 45, 46, 49, 53, 68, 81,
     123, 194

J

Japanese cars 90, 97, 144

K

Kelley Blue Book 35

L

lease return 45
lender 73, 74, 105
lien 44, 66, 192
low oil pressure 154

M

manual transmission 9, 96, 173
mechanic 4, 7, 20, 21, 34, 52, 54, 78, 81, 83, 86, 87,
     90, 93, 102, 115, 116, 131, 134, 139, 140, 151, 163,
     166, 171-173, 178, 179, 183, 184, 188-194, 196
mechanical failure 54, 140
miles per dollar 104, 109, 110, 112
mini-vans 76, 89

N

National Automobile Dealers 35
new car 6, 11, 12, 15, 16, 23, 28, 42, 54-57, 60, 64,
        67-69, 74-77, 79-91, 95, 99, 105, 106, 108, 114-116,
        120, 122, 124, 126, 128-130, 137, 140, 193, 197,
        199, 200
new parts 61, 66, 136, 180

O

obsolescence 4, 113, 114, 117, 119, 122, 126, 137
odometer 38, 81-84, 91, 102, 104, 105, 109, 138, 152,
        185, 187
oil pressure 153-158
older car 85-87, 101, 108, 127, 129, 130, 132-136, 186,
        187, 199
option 12, 14, 22, 26, 45, 64, 69, 72, 74, 80, 91-95,
        97-99, 101, 109, 114, 117, 120, 125, 131, 138
overhaul 96, 133, 135, 136, 139, 164, 177, 178-181,
        183, 188

P

paint 60-62, 79, 90, 91, 118, 140-143, 146-148, 179
paint repair 60, 61, 143
payment 12, 18, 72, 74, 75, 79, 86, 105-107, 192
planned obsolescence 4, 113, 114, 117, 122, 126, 137
power brakes 95
power door locks 97
power mirrors 94, 98
power seat 98, 150
power steering 27, 94, 104, 164, 171
power windows 80, 94, 97
private-party sale 4, 30
psychology 10

R

radiator 55, 102, 103, 153, 159, 160, 162, 185
radio 19, 99, 105, 122, 150, 194
rear defrost 94, 99
rebuilder 31, 41, 43, 44, 148, 180, 181

referral 24, 25, 52, 136, 165, 167, 190, 198
refinishing 60, 143
repaint 141, 142, 148
repair order 192, 193
replacement parts 194, 197
rural dealers 25

S

sales, private-party 4, 30
sales techniques 14-20
salvage pool 4, 40, 42-44
seats, power 98, 150
seats, split-bench 98
shade-tree, dealers 31
"spinning speedos" 83
sports car 13, 77, 78
station wagon 11, 76, 116
stereo systems 94
synchro 173, 174
system house 23

T

T-O house 16, 17, 24, 26
T-O system 16, 23
tilt wheel 94, 96
tires 19, 46, 86, 89, 103, 110, 146, 152, 169
title 20, 32, 43, 44, 64
total (wreck) 42, 43, 58, 63, 145
trade-ins 31, 35, 38, 41, 56, 67-70, 105
tune-up 86

U

upholstery 110, 138, 149
used part 188

W

warning lights 153-155
warranties 48, 51, 52, 53, 56, 113
windshield 88, 110, 142, 143, 148, 149, 185
wrecking yard 43, 184